Millennials
Go to College

Howe, Neil and Strauss, William
Millenials go to college, second edition
ISBN: 0-9712606-1-3
ISBN-13: 978-0-9712606-1-0

Table of Contents

Preface to the New Edition

Four years have elapsed since the publication of the First Edition of *Millennials Go to College*. In the 2002–03 academic year, colleges were startled by the arrival of a new generation of Millennials. Now, four years later, colleges are more likely to regard it as accomplished fact. Earlier this decade, so much was still breaking news—the "helicopter" moms, the over-programmed kids, the rising achievement of young women, the frenetic competition over college admissions, the vast numbers of young people who are careful and long-term planners, the rising media attention on all aspects of college life. Now, these have become familiar stories.

The greatest change over the last four years has been the intensification of the trends we identified in the First Edition, as later-born Millennial cohorts have been entering college. Back in 1990, when we published *Generations*, we envisioned that the Millennials would be a generation of trends that would accentuate with each passing cohort, and that the direction of these trends would often be the opposite of paths set by Boomers through the '60s and '70s. This is indeed occurring. It's nothing new, in the cycle of generations.

Meanwhile, new issues have emerged, from the ongoing rise of tuition and student borrowing to worries over male retention rates to the growing class divide between students who are affluent and those who are not to new parent demands for standards and accountability. College officials are noting the unprecedented influence of published institutional rankings and a rising anxiety about institutional reputation. The media attention that has followed Millennials up the age ladder is now focusing on recent graduates and entrants into the work force.

In many ways, these new issues reflect the arrival on campus of Millennials born closer to the midpoint of their generation. They also reflect shifts in parental cohorts. In the late '90s, many of the parents of collegians had themselves been students in the 1960s. Time has marched on, and admissions officials are starting to see prospective students arriving for campus visits accompanied by parents who had been in college in the 1980s: Generation Xers. Over the next several years, these early-wave Gen Xers will become a familiar parental fixture on campus.

The arrival of this new generation of parents will have substantial—and broadly foreseeable—consequences for higher education. The calls for standards, data, accountability, and personalized service will increase. Brand position, reputation, and the workplace performance of an institution's recent graduates will come under increased scrutiny. The parental attitudes and political impetus that brought the *No Child Left Behind* law to K-12 will make itself felt in academe. Some will applaud and embrace these trends and others will denounce and resist them—but they will become a fact of life for the nation's colleges and graduate schools as the '90s-born Millennials, and their Gen-X parents, pass through higher education.

Colleges are familiar with what we described in the First Edition as the Boomer "helicopter" parent. Coming soon is the era of the Gen-X "stealth fighter" parent, who will view each college's brand in terms of personal needs, family budgets, and cash value performance. In the new "What Comes Next" section that we prepared for this edition, we offer a number of suggestions for how colleges can deal not only with new parental trends, but with postgraduate job placements, graduate schools, alumni relations, and other trends we anticipate through the 2010s.

Four years ago, when we first inquired into parent and student attitudes by generation, we found very little data on these topics. To correct this, we joined with Crux Research and two generous sponsors—Chartwells Higher Education Dining Services and Datatel Incorporated—to conduct an extensive survey of generational relationships on today's campuses. This survey has generated what many colleges may consider to be very significant findings, useful for recruitment, admissions, financial aid, curricula, housing and food, career counseling, and other student services. We present summary findings of the Chartwells 2006 College Student Survey and the Datatel 2006 College Parent Survey in this edition. Information about how to acquire the full research report is available at *www.lifecourse.com*. In addition to the general research report, each of the study's sponsors provided Crux Research with a set of questions specific to their respective fields. More information on the analysis of these questions may be obtained from the contacts listed at that website.

In preparing this expanded Second Edition, we were immensely assisted by a number of very able and dedicated people. We thank Jim Graham, for his cover design and book layout, making the book an enjoyable read; Victoria Hays, for her help with countless details that go into tasks like these; Rick Delano, for his marketing acumen; John Geraci and his associates at Crux Research, for their path-breaking data collection and analysis; and, especially, Reena Nadler, our writing assistant, who has done so much to make the new edition larger and better. A true Millennial, and a recent graduate of Swarthmore College, Reena has not only helped with lively prose, perceptive data analysis, and careful editing, but has also lent an authentic been-there-done-that perspective to most of the topics we address.

As Reena (and the many other recent college graduates with whom we have spoken) are quick to point out, their generation has already made its mark on America's campuses. Yet the lasting imprint is still to come. Colleges that try to "ride out" the trends of the Millennial era as though they were still in the 1990s will run the risk of damaging their brands to the point where their reputations may take decades to repair. Worse, they could provide a disservice to the young people they are dedicated to educating. Conversely, colleges that see what's coming, and plan accordingly, will have an extraordinary opportunity not only to bolster their reputation, but also to provide an education that will be worthwhile to students, to America, and to history.

Much is now at stake. Between now and 2025, the reputation of even the nation's most famous colleges, including the Ivies, will be more at risk and subject to rapid fluctuation than at any time in living memory.

Dramatic changes in collegiate reputations and rankings have occurred before in American history. Back in 1893, *Baedeker's Handbook to the United*

States, a guide for British travelers, included what may have been the first ranking of American Universities, based purely on public reputation. Among the nine "best-known" colleges of that era were Hamilton, Lafayette, and Miami of Ohio. Among the top ten colleges in the 2007 *U.S. News* rankings (actually eleven, because of a tie), only Williams, Amherst, and Wellesley were cited by Baedeker. The other eight were not. His list of "great technical schools" of the 1890s included Stevens Institute of Technology (Hoboken, N.J.) and Rose Polytechnic (now the Rose-Hulman Institute of Terre Haute, Indiana), but not Cal Tech. And which schools were said to have the best football teams? Yale, Harvard, and Princeton.

Times, and institutional rankings, have changed in the 114 years since Baedeker lent an ear to the academic gossip. The era around World War II altered reputations considerably—as did, to a lesser degree, the turbulent campus era of the Consciousness Revolution. Now the currents of generational change, combined with other factors, appear powerful enough to change those rankings again.

Over the next two decades, large currents of history could sweep across our nation and the world. As we have written in *The Fourth Turning*, the graver the national challenge in the years ahead, the sharper the national focus will become on the young women and men of the rising generation—and on the educators who serve them.

The next twenty years will not be easy times for the nation's colleges and universities. The public and private priorities of higher education could come into sharp relief—and conflict. In writing this Second Edition, it is our hope that our readers will manage their institutions wisely, thereby enhancing their legacies while empowering the young. Thus can American higher education continue to serve as the next generational link spanning the past, present, and future of our civilization.

William Strauss
Neil Howe
January, 2007

Preface to the Original Edition

The Millennial Generation has long interested us for personal as well as professional reasons. We are each the parent of two, in both cases a boy and girl.

We've been studying their generation since the days of its first preschoolers, back in the middle 1980s. When we wrote *Generations* over a dozen years ago, we described how the children then entering elementary school rode "a powerful crest of protective concern," how they were seen as "precious" by Boomer parents who wielded a "perfectionist approach to child nurture" in an adult world that was "rediscovering an affection and sense of responsibility for other people's children."

In 1990, when most youth assessments were downbeat, even grim, we forecast that as these new children passed through adolescence, "substance abuse, crime, suicide, unwed pregnancy will all decline."

When these trends all came to pass, we were not surprised. There are good reasons, rooted in how they were raised and in the rhythms of history, for why this occurred.

Again and again over the centuries, in America and elsewhere, new generations arise that both correct the trends set in motion by their parents and fill the role being vacated by their grandparents. It is happening again. That's what these leading-edge Millennials are doing with (and to) a "Boomer Generation" in midlife and a "G.I. Generation" deep in elderhood.

Two years ago, when we published *Millennials Rising*, we chose as a subtitle "The Next Great Generation"-partly because, as a group, they exhibit qualities not generally seen in American youth since today's "senior citizens"-who, as collegians, were confident, optimistic, team oriented, rule following, and eager to achieve. And just as today's elder Americans did in their own youth, Millennials are growing up seeing their needs and dreams climb to the top of the national agenda.

We wrote *Millennials Go to College* at the urging of many college administrators, deans, registrars, admissions officers, and faculty members who, after having read our books or heard our lectures, agreed with us that Millennials are in fact arriving-and have asked us what they should do.

In Part One, we summarize the basic facts about today's new collegiate generation. We explain its location in history in relation to older generations. We describe the seven core Millennial traits: *special, sheltered, confident, team-oriented, conventional, pressured,* and *achieving.*

In Part Two, we explain what each of these traits means for colleges and universities-for recruiting and admissions, campus life, and the classroom-and what awaits in the years ahead, in career counseling, graduate school, the alumni ranks, and the world at large.

By necessity, we can only cover so much ground here. For readers who wish to learn more, we recommend *Millennials Rising* (2000), which we published just as the much-celebrated high school "Class of 2000" was entering college.

If you would like to learn more about our historical method, to see what we've written about Millennials in earlier years, or to pursue your own research on generational topics, please see *Generations* (1991) and *The Fourth Turning* (1997). To learn what we wrote about Gen Xers when they were collegians and young adults, please see *13th-Gen* (1993), which we published when today's 30-year-olds were graduating from college.

We invite readers with comments or questions to contact us at authors@ lifecourse.com.

When you study the students who pass through educational institutions as a succession of generations, you notice how each generation trains the next in skills and values-and, in so doing, each makes a profound contribution to the ongoing march of civilization. From the time when Benjamin Franklin's generation taught Thomas Jefferson's, through the time when Woodrow Wilson's taught Franklin Roosevelt's, on to our own childhood, when the best and brightest Rosie the Riveters taught us, we can see how tightly the chain of human progress is tied to the teaching and learning of the arts and sciences.

The questions, "Why do we teach? What is education for?" are best answered when you view the current generation of students as future parents, scientists, generals, playwrights, leaders, artists, historians-and teachers. When we describe Millennials as a "next great generation," we speak not just of their ancestry but also of their destiny.

Whatever that destiny may be, these young people will someday look back and thank you, their educators, for the gifts you gave them that made it possible.

Neil Howe

William Strauss

October, 2002

1 | A New Generation Goes to College

"Meet the Millennials, and rejoice."

— ANNA QUINDLEN, NEWSWEEK (2000)

A New Generation
Goes to College

A new generational wave has been breaking across campuses in America.

Dating back to their first births in the early 1980s, you could see this Millennial Generation coming. Everywhere they've been, from bulging nurseries to the new "Baby on Board" minivans, from day-care to kindergarten to high school, they have changed the face of youth—and transformed every institution they've touched.

In the fall of 2000, the first Millennials came to college. Along with their intrusive parents. And the glare of the media. At this writing, some of these young women and men are in their third year of graduate and professional school, and a great many more are in the workplace.

The years ahead can be a new golden age for America's colleges and universities. So too will they be years of increased stress, scrutiny, security, accountability, tuition relief, and mainstream political activism of a kind that will seem oddly unfamiliar to most veteran Boomer activists.

It will not be an easy time. The nature of every college function, from admissions to campus life to the classroom to career counseling, will change dramatically. The doctrine of *in loco parentis*, thrown over by rebellious Boomers forty years ago, has already reemerged in a new community guise as the Boomers' own children have filled dorm rooms.

The pressure on resources will be enormous. During the Gen-X collegiate era of the 1980s and '90s, admissions were stable and costs controllable, tuitions and endowments were rising, and students hunkered down, their fringes more powerful than their core, on the whole attracting little public attention. During the Millennial collegiate era, through the remainder of this decade and the one to follow, admissions will be more volatile and costs more unpredictable, tuitions more restrained (and price competition flagrant), and endowments less reliable. The core of students will overpower the fringes, and, as a group, they will command far more public attention.

Millennials are smart, ambitious, incredibly busy, very ethnically diverse, and dominated by girls, to this point. They make decisions jointly with demanding parents ("copurchasing" a college) and believe in big brands (with "reputation" counting for a lot). They are very numerous, very intent on going to college, and look forward to planned career paths.

Through the coming decade, they will transform the university world as profoundly as the Boomers did in the 1960s—but in very different, even opposite, ways. As happened in the '60s, some universities will figure out the new generation, deal with it correctly, and rise in reputation—and others will not. Some universities will make wise budget decisions, deftly tailoring income and expenditure streams around the needs and tastes of the new generation—and others will not. Some will market their college product smartly to the new youth mindset and to the new parental mindset—and others will not.

The next two decades may well become one of those eras when the rise of a new generation coincides with a mood of global urgency and public action. This can elevate the role of higher education in preparing the nation's "best and brightest" and in laying out the blueprint for a better future. The last comparable era was the 1930s and 1940s, decades when the collegiate pecking order was reshuffled. It was through the war-winning collegians of those years that the enduring reputations of many of today's elite institutions were forged.

The stakes are just as high in this post-9/11 Millennial student era. Colleges and universities that figure it out, make wise tuition and budget choices, and market intelligently to today's youth, will be able to "re-brand" their reputations, leapfrog rivals—and, perhaps, join the top echelons of academe. In this coming era of accountability, those that fail to do so could fall in reputation, or worse.

Wherever you are in university life, you face a choice. You can ignore this breaking Millennial wave, by treating today's collegians as you did the last generation. You can resist it, by pursuing decades-old agendas. You can ride it, by adapting as fast as you can to new needs as they arise. Or you can *lead* this new youth wave, by embracing Millennials as they arrive in full force.

Change is in the air on today's college campuses.

In some ways, these are boom times for academia. Applications are way up, and many schools are finding they can become much more selective. But it is also a time of spreading uncertainty and unease. Colleges and universities find themselves spending more and more on public relations, mindful of how much their reputations and rankings seem to be in flux. The new students strike many faculty members as well prepared and unexpectedly eager to please, but also as pressured and reluctant to take creative chances. Every little controversy—a case of alcohol poisoning in a frat house, a professor who criticizes the War on Terrorism, a student who plagiarizes, a T.A. who is seen dating a student, an admissions department found to be using a quota or asking other schools about their scholarships—gets the white hot glare of national media attention.

What's going on here? Very simple. A new generation—the Millennial Generation—has been coming of college age.

Since infancy, this generation has been the object of intense parental and societal attention, in forms as diverse as "zero tolerance" drug rules to a powerful school reform movement to whole new areas of pro-child health, safety, and "values education" initiatives. Largely as a result of that attention, this generation is marked by character traits that separate it from Generation X. Many of these traits are extremely positive. These youths are confident and optimistic, they are team- and rule-oriented, and they work very hard. Rates of tobacco and alcohol use, violent crime, pregnancy, and suicide rates are all way down among today's teenagers, while SAT and ACT scores have been rising.

To be sure, all of these positive traits also have their shadow side. Along with a greater willingness to play by the rules comes a new tendency towards conformity. Along with high confidence and a feeling of preciousness comes a tendency towards risk aversion. Along with an elevated respect for institutions come high expectations of authority and "zero tolerance" for institutional failure—an attitude that this generation will apply with particular force to institutions of higher learning.

In many ways that please older Americans, and in some that do not, Millennials are recasting the youth mood in America. The arrival of the heart of this generation, the quite numerous cohorts born in the late 1980s and early '90s—along with their increasingly Gen-X parents—will trigger consequences that could be as profound (though very different) as those triggered by young Boomers in the 1960s.

To understand how and why this may be true, let's first ask:

Who are they?

Part One

Who They Are

2 | Meet the Millennials

"I have not found this generation to
be cynical or apathetic or selfish.
They are as strong and as decent
people as I have ever met."

— JON STEWART, COMMENCEMENT ADDRESS AT THE
COLLEGE OF WILLIAM AND MARY (2004)

Meet the Millennials

Meet the students. "It's very rare to get a student to challenge anything or to take a position that's counter to what the professor says. They are disconcertingly comfortable with authority," says Robert Wuthnow of today's new crop of college students. "They're eager to please, eager to jump through whatever hoops the faculty puts in front of them, eager to conform."

And meet the moms and dads—whom Wake Forest official Mary Gerardy coined as "helicopter parents," always hovering—ultra-protective, unwilling to let go, enlisting "the team" (physician, lawyer, psychiatrist, professional counselors) to assert a variety of special needs and interests.

Where once parents simply unloaded the station wagon at the start of orientation week, kissed good-bye, and drove home, now they linger for days—fussing, meddling, crying, and even ranting if they think their very special child isn't getting the very best of everything. When they don't get their way, some threaten to take their business elsewhere or sue.

Program Titles for Freshmen Parent Orientation
What Have You Done With My Child? – University of North Carolina at Wilmington
May They Follow Your Path and Not Your Footsteps – Ohio Northern University
Between Mothering and Smothering, Between Fathering and Bothering – University of Southern California

The Changing Face of Youth

Teachers, professors, military officers, and others who work with youth often pride themselves on being the first to notice generational change when it occurs. Yet even those in closest contact with the youth culture are sometimes confounded by both the direction and timing of such change. Usually, the mistake is to assume that next year's collegians will be like last year's, only a bit more so. Most of the time that's true, but every two decades or so such linear projections prove to be catastrophically mistaken.

Consider the following expectations for youth at various times during the postwar era:

The Silent Generation came as a surprise.

In 1946, about the time General George Marshall declared the nation's victorious troops to be "the best damn kids in the world," Americans braced for fresh ranks of organized collegians who would take the mass mobilizations of the New Deal and World War II to a higher level of activism. These new youths were expected to be just like the world-conquering generation just before them, different only in that they might carry familiar youth traits to a higher level.

This didn't happen. After the returning G.I.s flowed quickly into and out of the nation's campuses, everyone was surprised to learn that the next generation of "teenagers" seemed uninterested in conquering the world. They kept their heads down, worried about their "permanent records," and planned on early marriages and long careers with big organizations.

Rather than change the system, the new collegians wanted to work within it. Looking back, historian William Manchester wrote, "[N]ever had American youth been so withdrawn, cautious, unimaginative, indifferent, unadventurous—and silent.... They waited so patiently for everything that visitors to college campuses began commenting on their docility."

Boomers came as a surprise.

By the early 1960s, Americans had grown used to talking about a "Silent Generation" of college students. As experts looked ahead to the onrushing bulge of children known as the "baby boom" who were about to arrive at college, they foresaw a new corps of technocratic corporatists, a Silent Generation to the next degree, even more pliable and conformist than the gray flannel "lonely crowd" right before them. "Employers are going to love this generation," Cal-Berkeley's Clark Kerr declared in 1959. "They are going to be easy to handle. There aren't going to be any riots."

Events, to say the least, turned out otherwise. Remarkably, none of the biggest-name social scientists—not even Erik Erikson or Margaret Mead—saw a hint of the youth explosion that was about to shake America.

Generation X came as a surprise.

Let's move forward another twenty years. Around 1980, experts in youth fields accepted the Boomers as the new norm for adolescent attitudes and behavior. The question was soon raised: What, they asked, would come from the next crop? These were the "Baby Busters" who had no memories of the assassination of John Kennedy and no clear impression of Woodstock, Vietnam, or even Watergate. What would they be like? Once again, the expectation was linear, that these youths would be like Boomers, only more so. Demographic forecasters suggested that the teens in the 1980s and 1990s would be more ideological, "holistic," and morals-driven—extending what *American Demographics* termed "an ongoing trend away from material aspirations toward non-materialistic goals."

Those predictions were rudely overturned when the scrappy, pragmatic, and free-agent Gen-X persona emerged a few years later. Disco gave way to MTV, soul to hip hop, Robin Williams to Tom Cruise. Long-haired ideologues were replaced by mohawked punks, suicidal grunge stars, goateed gamers, professional soldiers, gangsta rappers, and business school "power tools." The journey was no longer the reward; instead winning was "the only thing." College professors were confronted with students whose most piercing question seemed to be, "Is this on the test?" Once again, institutions that serve youth—from colleges to employers to the armed services—were thrown into disarray.

Millennials are coming as a surprise. Today, another twenty years have passed, and yet another generational change is on the doorstep. As a group, Millennials are unlike any other youths in living memory. More numerous, more affluent, better educated, and more ethnically diverse than those who came before, they are beginning to manifest a wide array of positive social habits that older Americans no longer associate with youth, including a new focus on teamwork, achievement, modesty, and good conduct.

Yet most people's perception of youth (especially those who don't have regular contact with teens) still lags behind reality. As was true twenty, forty, and sixty years ago, a common adult view is that today's teens are like the prior batch (Generation X), taken to the next degree (alias, Gen "Y"). A study recently published in the academic journal, *Social Policy Research*, finds American adults take a dim view of the younger generation. Among the findings:

* Only 16 percent of adult Americans agree that people under the age of 30 share most of their moral and ethical values.

* The three most frequently reported topics of youth news on the local stations are crime victimization, accidents involving young people, and violent juvenile crime, accounting for nearly half of all youth coverage. Five other frequently reported topics are: property crimes committed by juveniles, domestic violence or sexual abuse, alcohol abuse, and individual health problems.

* When asked to comment on recent unbiased news items about teenagers, adults consistently overlooked the positive data (which dominated the story) and focused instead on the few negative trends.

The data are clear—and reflect a profound disconnect between the good news about today's teens and the adult misperception of them. According to a recent national survey, barely one adult in three thinks that today's kids, once grown, will make the world a better place. To believe the newspapers, you'd suppose our schools are full of teenagers who can't read in the classroom, shoot one another in the hallways, spend their loose change on tongue rings, and couldn't care less who runs the country.

Part of this phenomenon is due to the tendency of people to be positive about their own lives and families (and the young people they know personally) while being very negative about the state of America in general (and youth in general). When asked about their parenting skills, parents give themselves an A or B—but give all other parents a D or F.

How depressing. And how wrong.

Look closely at youth indicators, and you'll see that attitudes and behaviors among today's youth represent a sharp break from Generation X, and are running exactly counter to trends launched by the Boomers. Across the board, Millennials are challenging the dominant and negative stereotype.

Are they pessimists? No. They're optimists. Nine in ten describe themselves as "happy," "confident," and "positive." Teen suicide rates are trending downward for the first time since World War II. A rapidly decreasing share of teenagers worry about violence, sex, or drugs, and a rapidly increasing share say that growing up is easier for them than it was for their parents.

Are they rule-breakers? No. They're rule-followers. Over the past

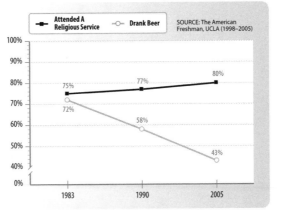

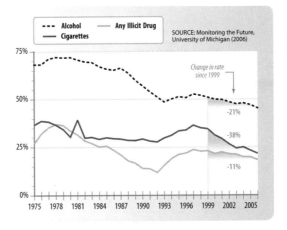

◄ Figure 2

Share of Kids Aged 12-17 having Specified Drug within Last Month, 1979 to 2000

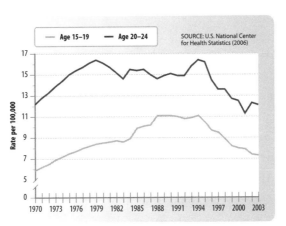

◄ Figure 3

Suicide Rates for Youth, Aged 15-19 and 20-24, 1970 to 2003

Figure 4 ▶

Serious Violent
Crime, Rate of
Offenders and
Victims Aged 12–
17, 1980 to 2004

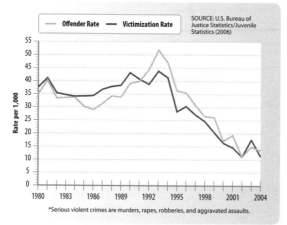

Serious violent crimes are murders, rapes, robberies, and aggravated assaults.

Figure 5 ▶

Share of High
School Students
from 1991 to
2005 Who Report
Having…

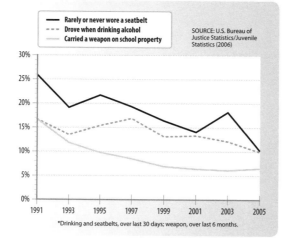

Drinking and seatbelts, over last 30 days; weapon, over last 6 months.

ten years, rates of violent crime among teens has fallen by 70 percent, rates of teen pregnancy and abortion by 35 percent, rates of high school sexual activity by 15 percent, and rates of alcohol and tobacco consumption are hitting all-time lows. As public attention to school shootings has risen, their actual incidence has fallen. Even including such shootings as Columbine, there have been fewer than half as many killings by students since 1998 (averaging fewer than fifteen per year) as there were in the early 1990s (over forty per year).

According to "Youth Risk Behavior" surveys run by the Centers for Disease Control and Prevention, risk taking is down across the board for high school students—in everything from binge drinking to not buckling your seatbelt.

Are they self-absorbed? No. From service learning to team grading, they are gravitating toward group activity. Twenty years ago, "community service" was unheard of in most high schools. Today, it is the norm, having more than tripled since 1984, according to the U.S. Department of Education. A 1999 Roper survey found that more teenagers blamed "selfishness" than anything else when asked about "the major cause of problems in this country."

Are they distrustful? No. They accept authority. Most teens say they identify with their parents' values, and more than nine in ten say they "trust" and "feel close to" their parents. A recent survey found 82 percent of teens reporting "no problems" with any family member—versus just 48 percent who said that back in 1974, when parents and teens were far more likely to argue and oppose one another's basic values. Half say they trust government to do what's right all or most of the

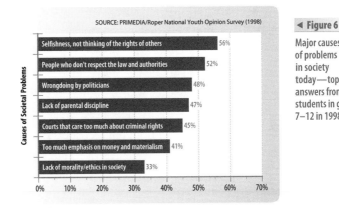

SOURCE: PRIMEDIA/Roper National Youth Opinion Survey (1998)

Causes of Societal Problems

- Selfishness, not thinking of the rights of others — 56%
- People who don't respect the law and authorities — 52%
- Wrongdoing by politicians — 48%
- Lack of parental discipline — 47%
- Courts that care too much about criminal rights — 45%
- Too much emphasis on money and materialism — 41%
- Lack of morality/ethics in society — 33%

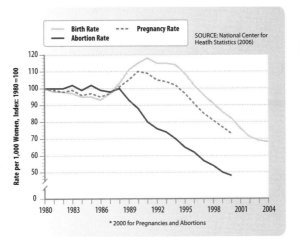

◀ **Figure 7**

Rates of Pregnancy, Abortion, and Birth for Girls Aged 15–17, 1980 to 2004*

Birth Rate   Pregnancy Rate   Abortion Rate

SOURCE: National Center for Health Statistics (2006)

Rate per 1,000 Women, Index: 1980 = 100

* 2000 for Pregnancies and Abortions

time—twice the share of older people answering the same question in the same poll. Large majorities of teens favor tougher rules against misbehavior in the classroom and society at large.

Are they neglected? No. They're the most watched-over generation in memory. The typical day of a child, 'tween, or teen has become a nonstop round of parents, relatives, teachers, coaches, babysitters, counselors, chaperones, minivans, surveillance cams, and curfews. Whether affluent or not, kids have become more closely managed. Since the mid-1980s, time diaries kept by kids and parents indicate that "unstructured activity" has been the most rapidly *declining* use of time among preteens.

Are they stupid? No. Since the late '80s, grade school aptitude test scores have been rising or flat across all subjects and all racial and ethnic groups. The number of high school students who take and pass an Advanced Placement test has more than doubled in the past ten years. Fully 73 percent of high school students today say they want a four-year college degree. A growing share is taking the SAT or ACT. Even so, the average score on these national tests is the highest in 30 years. Eight in ten teenagers say it's "cool to be smart."

Are they another "lost" generation? No. A better word is "found." Born in an era when Americans showed a more positive attitude toward children, the Millennials are the product of a birthrate reversal. During the Gen Xer childhood, planned parenting meant contraceptives; during the Millennial childhood, it has meant visits to the fertility clinic. In 1998, the number of U.S. children surged past its previous 1950s peak, and over the next decade, college freshman enrollment is due to grow by over twenty-five thousand per year. That means, each year, an extra army of freshmen four times larger than the incoming class at Ohio State.

Figure 8 ▶

Number of AP Exams with Grade of 3, 4, or 5, in all U.S. Public Schools

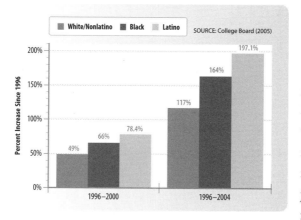

Generational Location in History

One way to define a generation's location in history is to think of a turning point in the national memory that its earliest birth cohorts just missed. Boomers, for example, are the generation whose eldest members have no memory of VJ Day. Gen Xers are the generation whose eldest members have no memory of John Kennedy's assassination. Millennials are the generation whose eldest members have no memory of Ronald Reagan's "Morning in America" election—that is, of an America still obsessed with stagflation, the Cold War, and "malaise."

Let's trace the historical location of each of the generations described earlier.

Seven U.S. Generations and Nearly 120 Birthyears

Except for many Boomers (who assume they've got the landscape mapped), when you talk generations, the first thing most folks want to know is: Where do I fit? This table puts the Millennials, their five predecessor generations, and the generation that will follow them, into perspective. Think about your own family—your parents, your favorite aunt or uncle, your youngest brother, your great-grandmother. When were they born, and how did their generational membership shape them? Then think about some individuals who have inspired you—movie stars, great writers, even political leaders—and speculate whether they have ended up carrying out a key part of their own generation's "script."

The Lost Generation (Born 1883–1900) had to grow up fast—amidst urban blight, unregulated drug use, "sweat shop" child labor, and massive immigration. As children, their violence, independence, and low educational achievement worried parents. As twentysomethings, they were brassy flappers, union scabs, expatriate novelists, and nihilist "flaming youth." They also pioneered entire economic sectors—supermarkets, roadside commerce, radio and aviation—that we take for granted today. After surviving a Great Depression that hit during their peak earning years, they slowed down and delivered pugnacious midlife leadership during World War Two. As crusty "Norman Rockwell" elders, they distrusted public power, gave generously to their world-conquering juniors, and asked remarkably little for themselves. *Louis Armstrong, Irving Berlin, Al Capone, Raymond Chandler, Amelia Earhart, Ernest Hemingway, the Marx Brothers, Dorothy Parker, George Patton, Harry Truman, Mae West.*

The G.I. Generation (Born 1901–24) enjoyed a "good kid" reputation as the beneficiaries of new playgrounds, scouting clubs, vitamins, and child-labor restrictions. They came of age with the sharpest rise in schooling ever recorded. As young adults, their uniformed corps patiently endured the Depression and heroically conquered foreign enemies. In a midlife subsidized by the G.I. Bill, they built suburbs, invented vaccines, plugged missile gaps, and launched moon rockets. Their unprecedented grip on the Presidency (1961 through '92) began with the New Frontier, Great Society, and Model Cities, but wore down through Vietnam, Watergate, and budget deficits. As senior citizens, they safeguarded their "entitlements" but had little influence over culture and values. *Walt Disney, Judy Garland, Alex Haley, Katharine Hepburn, John Kennedy, Ray Kroc, Ann Landers, Charles Lindbergh, Ronald Reagan, John Steinbeck.*

The Silent Generation (Born 1925–42) grew up as the suffocated children of war and Depression. They came of age just too late to be war heroes and just too early to be youthful free spirits. Instead, this early marrying "lonely crowd" became the risk-averse technicians and professionals as well as the sensitive rock 'n' rollers and civil rights advocates of a post-Crisis era—an era in which conformity seemed to be a sure ticket to success. Midlife was an anxious passage for a generation torn between stolid elders and passionate juniors. Their surge to power coincided with fragmenting families, cultural diversity, institutional complexity, and too much litigation. They are entering elderhood with unprecedented affluence, a hip style, and a reputation for indecision. *Shirley Temple, Bill Cosby, Nora Ephron, Martin Luther King, Jr., Richard Cheney, Sandra Day O'Connor, Paul Simon, Colin Powell, Dan Rather, Nancy Pelosi.*

The Boom Generation (Born 1943–60) grew up as indulged youth during an era of community-spirited progress. As kids, they were the proud creation of postwar optimism, Dr. Spock rationalism, and Father Knows Best family order. Coming of age, however, Boomers loudly proclaimed their antipathy to the secular blueprints of their parents; they demanded inner visions over outer, self-perfection over thing-making or team-playing. The Boom "Awakening" climaxed with Vietnam War protests, the 1967 "summer of love," inner-city riots, the first Earth Day, and Kent State. In the aftermath, Boomers appointed themselves arbiter of the nation's values and crowded into such "culture careers" as teaching, religion, journalism, marketing and the arts. During the '90s, they trumpeted values, touted a "politics of meaning" and waged scorched-earth culture wars. *Bill and Hillary Clinton, George W. and Laura Bush, Oprah Winfrey, Bill Gates, Condoleezza Rice, Tom Hanks, Meryl Streep, Rush Limbaugh, Katie Couric, Steven Spielberg.*

Generation X (Born 1961–81) survived a hurried childhood of divorce, latchkeys, open classrooms, and devil-child movies. They came of age curtailing the earlier rise in youth crime and fall in test scores—yet heard themselves denounced as so wild and stupid as to put The Nation At Risk. As young adults navigating a sexual battlescape of AIDS and blighted courtship rituals, they dated and married cautiously. In jobs, they have em-braced risk and prefer free agency over loyal corporatism. From grunge to hip-hop, their culture has revealed a hardened edge. Politically, they have leaned toward pragmatism and non-affiliation, and many would rather volunteer than vote. Widely criticized as "slackers," and facing a Reality Bites economy of declining young-adult living standards, they have embodied the "resilience" of post-9/11 America and have matured into one of the most dynamic generations of entrepreneurs in U.S. history. *Barack Obama, Julia Roberts, Mark Andreessen, Jon Stewart, Jodie Foster, Michael Jordan, Tom Cruise, Michael Dell, Johnny Depp, Quentin Tarantino, Ann Coulter.*

The Millennial Generation (Born 1982–200?) first arrived when "Baby on Board" signs appeared. As abortion and divorce rates ebbed, the popular culture began stigmatizing hands-off parental styles and recasting babies as special. Child abuse and child safety became hot topics, while books teaching virtues and values became best-sellers. By the mid-'90s, politicians were defining adult issues (from tax cuts to PBS funding to Internet access) in terms of their effects on children. Hollywood has replaced cinematic child devils with child angels; the media has cordoned off child-friendly havens; educators speak of standards and cooperative learning. As the leading edge of this generation now graduates from colleges and carefully starts careers under the wings of protective parents, rates of community service and voting among young adults are surging. *Ashley and Mary-Kate Olsen, Sarah and Emily Hughes, Raven-Symone, Mark Zuckerberg, Lindsay Lohan, Danica Patrick, LeBron James, Amanda Bynes, Michelle Wie, Hilary Duff, Freddie Adu, Kelly Clarkson, Haley Joel Osment, Megan Kanka*

The Homeland Generation (Born 200?) may be arriving now. These will be the babies born roughly through the mid 2020s. Their nurturing style will be substantially set by Gen Xers, but half of their parents will be Millennials. It is still too early to set their first birthyear; this will become clear in time.

The Silent arrived during the Great Depression and World War II, events they witnessed through the eyes of childhood, tending their Victory Gardens, while the next-older (G.I.) generation built and sailed in the Victory Ships that won the war.

Boomers arrived during the "Great American High" that followed the war, a childhood era of warmth and indulgence that marked them forever as a "postwar" generation, while the next-older Silent compliantly entered the suburban and corporate world.

Gen Xers arrived during the "Consciousness Revolution," amid the cultural turbulence of the Boomers' young adulthood.

Millennials arrived during the recent era of the "Culture Wars," while Gen Xers embarked on their young-adult dot-com entrepreneurialism.

America could now be entering a new post-9/11 era. How the War on Terror will affect Millennials over time as they become young adults, is a matter of speculation. So far, the mood is reinforcing several Millennial traits and desires that were already apparent—including their orientation toward personal safety, family closeness, community action, applied technology, and long-term planning.

Millennials live in a world that has taken trends Boomers recall from their childhood and turned them upside down. Boomers can recall growing up with a homogenizing popular culture and wide gender-role gap in an era when community came first and family stability was strong (though starting to weaken). Millennials have grown up with a fragmenting pop culture and a narrow gender-role gap in an era when individuals came first and when family stability was weak (though starting to strengthen).

As a postwar generation, Boomers arrived just when conforming, uniting, and turning outward seemed the nation's logical priority. As a post-awakening generation, Millennials began to arrive just when diversifying, atomizing, and turning inward seemed preferable. Such reversals reflect a fundamental difference in the two generations' location in history.

Millennials also represent a sharp break from Generation X. Gen Xers can recall growing up as children during one of the most passionate eras of social dissent and cultural upheaval in American history, an era in which the needs of children were often overlooked or discounted. This has left a deep impression on most of today's young Gen-X adults.

But Millennials can recall none of it. They have no personal memory of the ordered Cold War world (when only large and powerful governments had weapons of mass destruction). They only know about a post-Cold War era of multilateral confusion and power vacuums (when terrorists and rogue states are seeking these weapons). This generation has been shaped by such formative collective experiences as Columbine, the 2000 election, 9/11, Hurricane Katrina, and the Wars in Afghanistan and Iraq. In all of these instances, the real danger seems to come not from out-of-control institutions, but mostly from out-of-control individuals, or small groups of conspirators, who have become a menace to humanity because national or global institutions are not strong enough even to monitor them.

How Boomers and Gen Xers have responded to their own location in history is a story that is mostly written, a story replete with ironies and paradoxes. How Millennials will respond to theirs is a drama waiting to unfold. Yet if you know what to look for and why, certain themes in this drama can be anticipated, and their implications pondered.

How Every Generation Rebels

Over 150 years ago, Alexis de Tocqueville observed that, in America, "each generation is a new people." The question arises: Does some pattern or dynamic determine how each generation will be new?

Yes.

Three basic rules apply to any rising generation in nontraditional societies, like America, that allow young people some freedom to redefine what it means to be young, and to direct society according to their own inclinations—in other words, to "rebel."

First, each rising generation breaks with the styles and attitudes of the young-adult generation, which no longer function well in the new era.

Second, it corrects for what it perceives as the excesses of the current midlife generation—their parents and leaders—sometimes as a protest, other times with the support of parents and leaders who seek to complement their own deficiencies.

Third, it fills the *social role* being vacated by the departing elder generation, a role that now feels fresh, functional, desirable, and even necessary for a society's well-being. Through the living memory of everyone else, this dying generation has filled a social role so firmly as to prevent others from claiming it. Now, with its passing, this role is available again to the young.

When you apply these rules to the generational dynamic in America, you can see what's been happening, and will continue to happen even more powerfully, with Millennials.

Millennials will rebel against Gen-X styles and attitudes, correct for Boomer excesses, and fill the role vacated by the G.I.s.

Stylistically, today's teens are breaking with today's thirtyish Gen Xers and the whole "X" (and "X-treme") attitude. Expect peer networks instead of free agents, political action instead of apathy, technology to elevate the community and not the individual, on-your-side teamwork in place of in-your-face 'tude.

Gen Xers in their late twenties and thirties often regard themselves as the trend-setters of the teen culture, but often they know little about what actually goes on there. People that age are usually too old to have teens as siblings and too young to have teens as children. So they fall out of touch and, in time, a new batch of teens breaks with their culture. This happened in the early 1960s, again in the early 1980s, and it's starting to happen again.

Meanwhile, Millennials will correct for what teens see as the excesses of today's middle-aged Boomers: narcissism, impatience, iconoclasm, and a constant focus on talk (usually argument) over action. In their "rebellion," Millennials will opt for the good of the group, patience, conformism, and a new focus on deeds over words. When they argue among themselves, they will value finding consensus more than being right. When they argue with older generations, they will try to persuade by showing how more than by explaining why. Unlike Boomers, Millennials won't bother spending three days at a retreat to figure out how to rewrite a mission statement. With adults of all philosophical stripes yearning for "community," the Millennial solution will be to set high standards, get organized, team up, and actually create a community.

The third rule of rebellion may be the key to understanding not just what Millennials are now doing, but where they see their clearest path in the years ahead.

Remember those whom Tom Brokaw christened the "greatest generation"— the ones who pulled America out of Depression, conquered half the globe as soldiers, unleashed nuclear power, founded suburbia, and took mankind to the moon. The most important link this "G.I. Generation" has to today's teens is in the void they leave behind: No other adult peer group possesses anything close to their upbeat, high-achieving, team-playing, and civic-minded reputation. Sensing this social role unfilled, today's adults have been teaching these (G.I.) values to Millennials, who now sense the G.I. "archetype" as the only available script for correcting or complementing the Boomer persona.

Today's Millennial teens often identify the G.I.s as their grandparents. When asked in surveys to assess the reputations of older generations, Millennials say they have a much higher opinion of G.I.s and a somewhat lower one of Gen Xers than they do of any generation in-between—Boomers (the children of the postwar American High) or the Silent (the children of World War II). Many speak glowingly about G.I.s as men and women who "did great things" and "brought us together as a nation."

In a 2001 *Atlantic Monthly* cover story, David Brooks labeled Millennials "Organization Kids," a tacit reference to the original G.I. "Organization Man," and about as far as you can get from the "Bourgeois Bohemians" Brooks finds so common among the middle-aged.

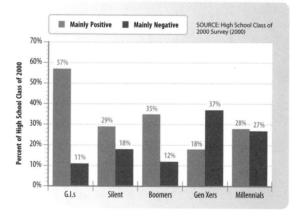

◀ **Figure 9**

High School Class of 2000, Opinion on Generational Reputations

Today's teens don't rebel against midlife Boomers by being hyper-Xers—not when the oldest Xers are themselves entering their mid-forties. They rebel by being G.I. redux, a youthful update of the generation against which the

Boomers rebelled thirty years ago. No one under the age of 70 has any direct memory of teens or twentysomethings who are G.I. in spirit. Millennials are, and will be. That's why what's around the cultural corner is so profound that it might better be called a youth revolution. Rebellions peter out—but revolutions produce long-term social change.

3 | Life Before College

"We like to let people in on a little secret. These kids are less likely to take drugs, less likely to assault somebody else, less likely to get pregnant, and more likely to believe in God."

— VINCENT SHIRALDI, JUSTICE POLICY INSTITUTE (2000)

Life Before College

The change came in 1982. The February 22, 1982 issue of *Time* offered a cover story about an array of thirtysomething Boomers choosing (finally) to become moms and dads. That same year, bright yellow "Baby on Board" signs began popping up in station-wagon windows.

Around Christmas of 1983, adult America fell in love with Cabbage Patch Kids—a precious new doll, harvested pure from nature, so wrinkly and cuddly-cute that millions of Boomers wanted to take one home to love. Better yet, why not a genuine, live Millennial?

The era of the wanted child had begun.

In September 1982, the first Tylenol scare led to parental panic over trick-or-treating. Halloween suddenly found itself encased in hotlines, advisories, and statutes—a fate that would soon befall many other once-innocent child pastimes, from bicycle-riding to BB guns.

A few months later came national hysteria over the sexual abuse of toddlers, leading to dozens of adult convictions after what skeptics liken to Salem-style trials.

All the while, new books (*The Disappearance of Childhood, Children Without Childhood, Our Endangered Children*) assailed the "anything goes" parental treatment of children since the mid-1960s. Those days were ending, as the family, school, and neighborhood wagons began circling.

The era of the protected child had begun.

Through the early 1980s, the national rates for many behaviors damaging to children—divorce, abortion, violent crime, alcohol-intake, and drug-abuse—reached their postwar high-water mark. The well-being of children began to dominate the national debate over most family issues: welfare, latch-key households, drugs, and pornography.

In 1983, the federal _Nation at Risk_ report on education blasted grade-school students as "a rising tide of mediocrity," prompting editorialists to implore teachers and adults to do better by America's next batch of kids.

In 1984, "Children of the Corn" and "Firestarter" failed at the box office. Hollywood was astonished, since these were merely the latest installments in a child-horror film genre that had been popular and profitable for well over a decade, ever since "Rosemary's Baby" and "The Exorcist." But not as many parents wanted to see them now. Instead, they preferred a new kind of movie ("Baby Boom," "Parenthood," "Three Men and a Baby") about adorable babies, wonderful tykes, and adults who improve their lives by looking after them.

The era of the worthy child had begun.

In 1990, the Wall Street Journal and New York Times had headlines—"The '60s Generation, Once High on Drugs, Warns Its Children" and "Do As I Say, Not As I Did"—that would have been unimaginable a decade earlier. Polls showed that Boomer parents did not want their own children to have the same freedom with drugs, alcohol, and sex that they once enjoyed.

By the early '90s, elementary-school kids were in the spotlight. During the Gulf War Super Bowl of 1991, children marched onto the field at halftime amid abundant media coverage (unseen during the Vietnam War) of the children of dads serving abroad.

Between 1986 and '91, the number of periodicals offered to young children doubled. Between 1991 and '94, the sale of children's music also doubled. In tot-TV fare, "Barney and Friends" (featuring teamwork and what kids share in common) stole the limelight from "Sesame Street" (featuring individualism and what makes each kid unique).

What Millennials
Don't Remember

Each year, at Beloit college, Professor Tom McBride and his colleagues have drawn up the "Beloit College Mindset List" (see www.beloit.edu), a list of the ways in which the new batch of college freshmen see the world differently than older Americans do. "We assemble this list out of a genuine concern for our first-year students, and as a reminder to the faculty of the gap that may exist between generations," the authors note. "Education is the best remedy for the situation, but we start out with varying points of reference and cultural touchstones."

Members of the class of 2010, entering college in the fall of 2006, were mostly born in 1988. The Beloit list notes that, for these students, Billy Carter, Lucille Ball, Gilda Radner, Billy Martin, Andy Gibb, and Secretariat have always been dead. The following is a sample of a few of the seventy items on the Beloit list.

- The Soviet Union has never existed and therefore is about as scary as the student union.

- They have known only two presidents.
- There has always been only one Germany.
- A stained blue dress is as famous to their generation as a third-rate burglry was to their parents'.
- Reality shows have always been on television.
- They have always been able to watch wars and revolutions live on television.
- Professional athletes have always competed in the Olympics.

During 1996, major-party nominees Dole and Clinton dueled for the presidency in a campaign full of talk about the middle school children of "soccer moms."

The next year, Millennials began to make an impression on the pop culture. Thanks to the Spice Girls, Hanson, and others, 1997 ushered in a whole new musical sound—happier, brighter, and more innocent. "They like brands with heritage. Contrived, hard-edged fashion is dead. Attitude is over," MTV president Judy McGrath said of her company's new teen interns. "They like what's nice and fun in fashion and sports. They like the Baby Gap ads; they're simple and sweet."

The era of the perfected child had begun.

Those MTV interns were late-wave Gen Xers, born a little before 1980. But the big change—the revolution in youth—was coming from the 1982-86 birth cohorts. Other key trends have followed Millennials who were born later in the 1980s. Test scores, which improved somewhat for the first cohorts, have improved even more among today's heavily homeworked, super-tested 'tweens who are now in middle school or entering high school. By the time these young people reach college age, campuses will be a hotbed of Millennial styles, and the true Millennial persona will reveal itself in full force. By the time kids born in the early '90s show up at college, the era of Boomer parenthood will be closing. Most of the parents of the later-born half of the Millennial Generation will be Gen Xers.

Boomers started out as the objects of loosening child standards in an era of conformist adults. Millennials have started out as the objects of tightening child standards in an era of nonconformist adults. By the time the last Millennials come of age, they could become the best-educated youths in American history, and the best-behaved young adults in living memory. But they may also have a tendency toward copying, consensus, and conformity that educators will want to challenge, as well as many other character traits that will require broad changes in the academy.

Through the late 1990s, the first wave of these much-watched children passed through high school, accompanied by enormous parental, educational, and media fascination—and headlines, not all of them positive. After the April 1999 Columbine tragedy was replayed again and again on the news, the adult absorption with Millennial safety, achievement, and morality reached a fever pitch.

Eighteen months after Columbine, these wanted, protected, worthy, perfected children began entering college.

Twenty years ago, the arrival of Generation X on campus took many institutions of higher learning by surprise. Professors and administrators began noticing that incoming students were less interested in the protest movements that had driven college life throughout the '60s and '70s. The level of intellectual engagement seemed to drop precipitously. Students no longer debated professors about the curriculum. Why bother with what anyone else thinks, when you can simply vote with your feet, switch classes, and stick with your own niche?

The Gen-X attitude toward knowledge was more instrumental than that of Boomers. In history classes, students were less likely to ask about which wars were moral than about how you win one. The most highly motivated students gathered in professional schools, where the object was less to change the world than to enable grads to make a lot of money. A good student was one who could get the best transcript with the least possible expenditure of effort—a bottom-line focus that Gen Xers maintained as entry-level workers in the late '80s and '90s, with wondrous consequences for the economy's productivity.

Think about all of the ways that institutions of higher learning had to adjust to fit this style of student. *In loco parentis*, already under assault during the '60s and '70s, virtually disappeared. Pass/fail grading options became available for many if not most classes, and core curricula requirements were relaxed. Widespread use of drugs and alcohol forced colleges and universities to build new relationships with local police. Speech codes were enacted to counter uncivil discourse. Large, school-wide events became less common, as cynicism about school spirit and campus community spread. Students took longer to earn their degrees.

College clientele changed as well. More foreign, older, and "continuing education" students were enrolled. To meet shifting demands driven by changing economic conditions, business and law schools expanded, while science and engineering departments were increasingly the province of international students.

Now, with the arrival of the Millennials, campus life is undergoing another transformation. Policies that were needed for college students in the '80s and '90s have become inappropriate. Instead, in the current decade, college administrators have been adjusting their institutions to a new crop of students who have been (and are):

* Close to their parents
* Focused on grades and performance
* Intensely focused on the college admissions process
* Packing their resumes with extracurricular and summer activities
* Eager to volunteer for community service
* Talented in digital-mobile technologies
* Capable of multitasking and interested in interactive learning
* More interested in math and science, relative to the humanities
* Insistent on secure, regulated environments
* Respectful of norms and institutions
* Conventionally minded, verging on conformist-thinking

* Ethnically diverse, but less interested than their elders in questions of racial identity
* Majority female, but less interested than their elders in questions of gender identity

They also are very numerous and very intent on going to college, which is making these trends all the more consequential.

In the fall of 2004, the first Millennials graduated from colleges. They then began entering law schools, medical schools, and other post-graduate programs—and the ranks of collegiate alumni. As they have flooded into the highest student reaches of academe, every aspect of university life has begun revealing a new young-adult mindset.

4 | Millennials By the Numbers

"Most teenagers are making good choices—focusing on their futures and saying no to anything that would jeopardize their dreams."

— DONNA SHALALA, FORMER SECRETARY OF HEALTH AND HUMAN RESOURCES (2000)

Millennials By the Numbers

To demographers and economists, each new generation brings with it a new batch of numbers and trend lines. One good test of whether we can draw an accurate qualitative profile of a generation is whether this profile matches the numbers. Let's take a new look at Millennials by the numbers: their size, their diversity, the hours they play, the brands they buy, the reasons they work, and the prices they (and their families) pay for college.

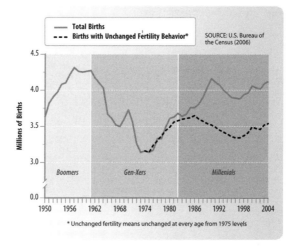

SOURCE: U.S. Bureau of the Census (2006)

◄ **Figure 10**

Total U.S. Births, in Millions, 1950 to 2004

The Baby Boomlet

The best-known single fact about the Millennial Generation is that it is large. Already, America has well over ninety million Millennials. By the time future immigrants join their U.S.-born peers, this generation will probably top one hundred million members, making it nearly a third bigger than the Boomers. In native births per birthyear (expected to average 3.9 million), Millennials will greatly exceed Gen Xers, edge out Boomers, and tower over every earlier generation in America.

Since most Millennials born in the 1980s are the children of Baby Boomers, the media often refers to them as America's new "Baby Boomlet" or "Echo Boom" generation. In two key ways, these terms are misleading. First, the 1990s-born Millennials—the larger half of the generation—are primarily the children of Gen Xers, not Boomers. And, second, these terms imply that the large number of Millennials is mainly a matter of arithmetic, as though a "baby boomlet" mechanically had to issue from "baby boom" parents. Yes, that happened, but the echo effect accounts for only a small part of the rise. Most of the birth bulge reflects higher fertility—the greater likelihood by the mid-'80s that the typical woman of childbearing age would have a baby. For the most part, what gave rise to the large number of Millennials was the passionate desire of their parents to bear and raise more of them.

The larger-than-expected size of this generation is therefore an extension of the early-'80s shift in adult attitudes toward children. The arrival of the first Gen Xers in the early '60s coincided with a sharp decline in the U.S. fertility rate and a society-wide aversion to children. And so it remained for the following twenty years, as small children seldom received positive media, while adults complained to pollsters about how family duties hindered their self-discovery. Children became linked to new adjectives: unwanted, at-risk, throwaway, homeless, latchkey.

By 1975, when annual births had plunged to barely three million—versus over four million in the late 1950s—newspapers talked about Gen Xers as America's new "Baby Bust" generation. Baby-market companies, like Gerber Products, were hit hard. Starting in 1977, annual births tilted back up again, slowly at first, and the baby industry began bouncing back. By the early 1980s, Gerber and the others were rescued by a floodtide of new babies, who also brought good cheer to the manufacturers of cribs, strollers, rockers, safety seats, PJs, dolls, safety gadgets, and toddler books and videos.

Most experts at the time contended that the late-'70s birth surge would be short lived, but they were in for a surprise. After leveling off at about 3.6 million during 1980-83, the national birth rate did not drift back down. Instead, it rose—to 3.8 million in 1987, 4.0 million in 1989, and 4.2 million in 1990. In many regions, hospital delivery rooms became overcrowded and pediatricians hard to find. During the 1990s, the annual number of births drifted below the 4.0 million benchmark, until 2000 produced another surge in the fertility of young (this time, Gen-X) women. Overall, Millennial births have been roughly 20 percent higher than if the fertility of women at each age had remained steady at mid-'70s rates.

During the 1960s and '70s, the era of Gen-X babies, adults went to great efforts not to produce children, driving up the demand for contraceptive technologies and for sterilization and abortion clinics. During the Millennial baby era, by contrast, adults have gone to great efforts to conceive and adopt babies. Sterilization rates, which rose sharply in the 1960s and '70s, plateaued in the middle '80s and have since fallen. The annual abortion rate, after ramping up during the Gen-X baby era, hit a peak in 1980 and declined steadily through most of the '80s and '90s. Meanwhile, the share of all births declared to be "unwanted" by their mothers has also declined—with an especially sharp drop in unwantedness by African-American mothers.

What's important about this "baby boomlet" is how sustained it became, and how it has reflected a resurgent adult desire to have kids. As a share of the population, America actually had more grade-school children during the tail-end years of the postwar

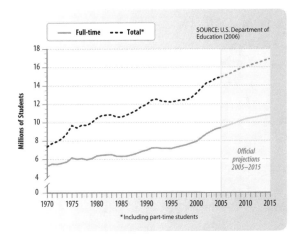

◀ Figure 11

Total Number of Students Enrolled in U.S. Institutions of Higher Learning, 1970 to 2015

baby boom than it does today. But back when those last Boomers were in elementary school, around 1970, the number of schoolchildren was trending downward—and steadily fewer adults wanted to bear them, make films or TV shows for them, or pay much public attention to them.

The first (mainly Boomer-parented) 1990 peak of the Millennial birth bulge has been rippling up the school age ladder for some time now. Primary schools felt it in the late 1990s, middle schools just after 9/11, and high schools are feeling it now. Colleges will draw students from these larger cohorts later this decade. The second (mainly Xer-parented) 2000 peak is just starting to enter elementary schools, and will hit colleges in the late 2010s.

The final birthyear of the Millennial Generation is yet to be determined. They may be the children who have no personal memory of 9/11, or perhaps some other generational boundary will emerge. Time will tell. Over the past two centuries in America, generations have ranged in length from seventeen to twenty-four years, a span that suggests that the final Millennials will be those born sometime between 1999 and 2006. The next batch of children, the Homeland Generation, will include children of Gen-X and Millennial parents—and will start arriving at college sometime around the year 2020.

Colors of the World

Millennials are the least Caucasian and most racially and ethnically diverse generation in U.S. history. As of 2006, non-whites and Latinos accounted for 41 percent of the twenty-three-or-under population, a share nearly two-thirds larger than for the Boomer age brackets, and nearly three times larger than for today's seniors.

Millennials have a much greater range of global diversity than Boomers did during their own college years. The issue of color can no longer be defined in clear black-white (or even black-white-Latino) terms. A class full of Millennial collegians, even when one looks just at American citizens, can include young women and men whose ancestors come from nearly every society on earth, including regions (Central and South America, Sub-Saharan Africa, the Arab

Figure 12 ▶

Minority* Share of Total Students Enrolled in U.S. Institutions of Higher Learning, 1976 to 2004

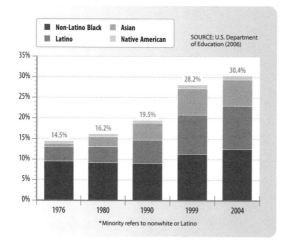

Non-Latino Black Asian
Latino Native American

SOURCE: U.S. Department of Education (2006)

14.5% 16.2% 19.5% 28.2% 30.4%

1976 1980 1990 1999 2004

*Minority refers to nonwhite or Latino

crescent, South Asia) that were far less represented on the campuses of the 1960s. The wide range of ethnic diversity is influencing many of the activities in which Millennials participate.

To this point, Millennials are less often immigrants themselves than the children of immigrants. In 2003, just fewer than 5 percent of Millennials were immigrants themselves, versus 17 percent of Gen Xers and 12 percent of Boomers. Yet one Millennial in five has at least one immigrant parent, and one in ten has at least one non-citizen parent. Containing more second-generation immigrants than any earlier twenty-year cohort group in U.S. history, Millennials embody the "browning" of American civilization.

Thanks to the Cold War's end, satellite news, porous national borders, and the Internet, they are also becoming the world's first generation to grow up thinking of itself, from childhood forward, as global. For Millennials, therefore, ethnicity is more often a question of mixed identity than of racial polarization. A variety of ethnic beauty pageants were held in 2005 and 2006 crowning young women as "Miss Liberia USA," "Miss Vietnam USA," and "Miss Ethiopia North America," among others.

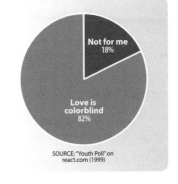

◄ **Figure 13**

Opinion on Interracial Dating

Indeed, American (and Canadian) students mark the leading edge of a new worldwide generation. Since World War II, the leading edges of new European generations have arrived roughly five years or so after those in America. Euro-teens still have more of an X than Millennial aspect, but some observers in Europe and Asia are describing the emergence of a Millennial-style shift among young teens. In Germany, these new kids have been called the *Null Zoff* ("no problem") generation—in Sweden, *Generation Ordning* ("ordered generation").

As always, America is expected to play a large role in determining how this rising generation is perceived around the world, just as it did with global Generation X. As Lee Siew Hua observed in the Malaysian *Straits Times*, "The Millennial Generation will in time produce a mightier imprint on American life and decency standards, and possibly globally, as long as the United States exports trends." Although generational patterns vary somewhat around the world, given each country's own particular history and culture, it is likely that most of today's 20-year-old foreign students may in fact be part of a different generation than 20-year-old American students. But that will probably not be true five years from now, and certainly not ten years from now.

Dating back to Emancipation, African-Americans have been an outsized cultural contributor to generational currents. In recent decades, we have seen this in civil rights (Silent), black power (Boomers), and hip-hop (Gen Xers). That contribution continues, albeit in new forms, with today's urban school-children, who are far more likely than suburbanites to learn by rote and jointly shout upbeat slogans like, "I'm going to succeed!" in the classroom.

Millennials are the first American generation in which Latinos clearly out-number African-Americans. With over half having at least one immigrant parent, many young Latinos face a future full of hard challenges: One-third lives in poverty, in substandard housing, and without health insurance. The rate at which Latinos in grades 10–12 drop out of school each year (nine per-cent) is much higher than the rate for non-Latinos (five percent). Problems are particularly acute for Latino boys, who have lower expectations for the future than their female counterparts. Yet many Latino pop icons provide a distinctly Millennial feel with upbeat lyrics, colorful clothes, dancing in cou-ples, and close family ties.

In 2006, a number of Latino teenagers took leadership roles in several of the "movimiente" marches on behalf of immigrants. The most prominent were not immigrants themselves, but rather the citizen children of non-citizen (and often undocumented) parents. Their use of digital-mobile technologies as organizing tools and the overall civic nature of the campaign—well behaved and demanding a stronger connection between their families and America's public institutions ("today we march, tomorrow we vote")—reflected the tone of this new generation as a whole.

Asian teens are also a rapidly growing presence. Propelled by cultures that honor filial duty and credentialed achievement, teens from Chinese, Indochinese, and Indian families have won a reputation among Millennials as stellar academic achievers—especially in math, science, and engineering, as well as in the fine arts. In most U.S. high schools today, they are hugely over-represented in honors and AP classes and among students with the highest GPAs and test scores. Aware that Asians often set the pace, other teens are motivated to work harder to keep up.

Both Latino and Asian youth are challenged by unfair stereotypes. Behind the image of the Latino "drop out" are teens who quit high school to help their families earn money or quit college because they are unwilling (less willing than whites, despite their lower income) to take out student loans to pay tuition. Behind the image of the Asian "nerd" are teens who have been taught by their families that to gain entry to the American establishment is a special privilege. With parents even more attached to "family values" than the white adult majority, both the Latino and Asian youth cultures are setting a distinctly Millennial tone--positive, team-playing, risk averse, and friendly--in schools and neighborhoods from Boston to San Diego.

In many respects, urban non-white youths—especially African-Americans—are bigger contributors to this generation's emerging persona than white youths. Ask yourself these questions: Which kids are more likely to be wearing school uniforms? Urban non-whites. Whose schools are moving fastest on back-to-basics drilling and achievement standards? Urban non-whites. Whose neighborhoods are producing the swiftest percentage decline in street murder, child poverty, teen pregnancy, and school violence? Urban non-whites.

A team of social scientists at Duke University has recently combined twenty-five key indicators of adolescent and teen well-being (everything from child poverty and abuse to teen crime and drug use) over the last twenty years into an aggregate annual "Youth and Child Well-Being Index." Not only does this Index show a dramatic upward thrust starting in 1994—just when Millennials began occupying adolescence—it also showed that the improvement for Latino and African-American minorities has been considerably steeper than for the white majority.

Regionally, the (mostly minority) urban areas have shown the steepest gains. The suburbs are in the middle. The (mostly white) rural areas have shown the slowest gains. In recent years, rural youths have shown the least decline or even a rise in the use of alcohol, cigarettes, marijuana, and many harder drugs (like methamphetamine). Their cultural tastes may also lag behind their peers elsewhere, to whom they may look for signals.

Figure 14 ▶
"Index of Child Well-Being" Duke University's Index of 28 Key Youth Indicators

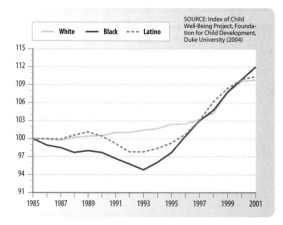

SOURCE: Index of Child Well-Being Project, Foundation for Child Development, Duke University (2004)

The unprecedented ethnic diversity and mixed-race aspect of this generation, combined with the fact that they are precursors of a new generation elsewhere in the world, makes them globally powerful.

Busy Around the Clock

Millennial teens and collegians may be America's busiest people.

Long gone are the old days of Boomer kids being shooed outside to invent their own games—or of Gen Xer kids being left "home alone" with a "self-care" guide. For most of today's small children, such a hands-off nurturing style would be considered dangerous, even abusive. For today's teens, unchaperoned events are far less likely—and, when they occur, can provoke a far greater outcry if anything bad happens. For today's collegians, it's unusual to have on-campus parties without wrist tags, "party associates" to monitor their fellow students' drinking (and driving), and occasional unscheduled check-ins from the campus police.

The new reality is structure, planning, and supervision, from kindergarten through college—and, perhaps, in the young-adult workplace. From 1991 to 1998, according to University of Michigan researchers, eighth and tenth graders showed sharp reductions in the share of those who engage "every day" or "at least once a week" in such open-ended youth activities as going to movies, cruising in cars and motorcycles, or walking around shopping malls. Vast majorities of high school seniors say they are more looked after and have less free time than their older brothers and sisters at the same age. During the 1990s, the sale of student day-planners soared from one million to fifty million. As 10-year-old Stephanie Mazzamaro told *Time* magazine: "I don't have time to be a kid."

In a survey on pre-school and elementary-school kids aged 3 to 12 — now aged 11 to 20 — comparisons of time diaries between 1981 and 1997 revealed a stunning 37 percent decline in the amount of "unstructured" free time, from 52 to 33 hours per week. Beyond Internet-use, here is where this time is going.

    ✳ **School:** *Up by 8.3 hours per week.* This is the single most expanded child activity. More kids aged 4 and 5 (known in earlier generations as "pre-schoolers") are now in school. More grade schools have early morning classes, after-school programs, "extra learning opportunity" programs, and summer school, which is now mandatory in many districts for kids who score low on certain tests or sought after by kids who want extra credits for the new year. Federal spending on after-school programs is growing rapidly, although 74 percent of elementary and middle school parents say they would pay for such programs out of their own pocket, if necessary.

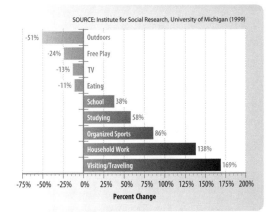

◄ **Figure 15**

Weekly Hours of Children Aged 3-12, by Activity Percent Change, from 1981 to 1997

    ✳ **Household chores:** *Up by 3.5 hours per week.* Many more chores are done by today's kids, either alone or (as with grocery-shopping) with a parent.

    ✳ **Personal care:** *Up by 3 hours per week.* Showering, hair care, tooth care, dressing, and other cosmetic items are taking more time.

    ✳ **Travel and visiting:** *Up by 2.5 hours per week.* This includes visits to non-custodial parents, who sometimes live in distant cities, or time spent in transit to soccer games, music lessons, and other scheduled events.

The young people who have grown up spending their time this way are now entering college. The bottom line is this: Today's rising generation is busy—and often not in ways that today's adults can recall from their own youth. Millennial children are less likely to spend time lying on their backs imagining stories as they clouds roll by, and more likely to spend time learning how to excel at standardized tests. They are less likely to play self-invented games with made-up rules, ending when they feel like it, and more likely to play on select teams with adult referees, professionalized rules, and published standings. Today's collegians are less likely to sunbathe idly on the campus green and more likely to hurry across it on the way to the computer lab (perhaps with an iPod in one ear and a cell phone in the other). They are less likely to play frisbee or toss a football around, and more likely to go to the gym to run on a treadmill—or stay in the dorm and play in elaborately organized videogame tournaments.

Teens as a Target Market

Thus far, over their brief collective lifespan, there has been much commercial interest in Millennials—how to make them watch an ad, how to make them buy, how to use them to make their parents buy. Driving this interest is in part their sheer numbers and the overall affluence of the '90s—but also a sudden awareness, among teen marketers, that generations matter. In the early '90s, marketers awoke to the realization that they had never fully targeted Gen-X, and they were determined not to let this mistake recur with the next batch of teens.

There's no question that, today, a lot more cash is being spent on young people than ever before, as anyone who has recently visited a typical teen bedroom can attest. The first wave of this generation has grown up during an era of surging prosperity—from the early 1980s through the year 2000—when there was only one mild recession and the Dow rose almost every year. Purchases by and for children aged 4 to 12 tripled over the 1990s, and teens hit their stride at the decade's end.

In recent years, however, parental worries, high youth unemployment, and growing indebtedness among college-bound teens seem to be dampening the spending fire. One youth marketing firm finds that the purchasing volume flowing through the hands of Americans aged 12 to 19 shot up from $153 billion in 1999 to $172 billion in 2001. Since then, it's been zigzagging back down again. In 2002, after 9/11, teen purchasing edged down to $170 billion; in 2003, back up to $175 billion; by 2005, back down to $159 billion.

Such figures must be interpreted with care. Whether a family is affluent or not, it is increasingly hard to tell where a kid's own spending stops and where spending on his or her behalf begins. In recent years, people of many age brackets have been spending more on children and teenagers—youths themselves, parents on their own kids, and grandparents and other non-parents on young friends and relatives. Many Americans worry that all this spending is spoiling young people, who have been raised in an era of nonstop affluence. But no one can say these kids are collectively neglected. Rightly or wrongly, adults are favoring this new generation by steering more money towards its wants, and by identifying its wants with their own.

At the moneyed end of the spectrum, there's truly no limit to what parents (Boomer parents in particular) are willing to spend on their children. Witness the boom in pricey summer camps (for which weekly bills can run to $2,000), lavish overseas teen travel adventures, teen-driven SUVs, and the daily crowds of rich Manhattan teens with Prada handbags and Versace clothes.

In the middle class, teens have been stocking up on enough electronic gear to fill every available inch of their bedrooms and dorm rooms, willingly paid for by parents who see this as a path to college and future success in a dot-com economy. Beyond that, major companies keep adding new product lines just for Millennials, from Kids' Aquafresh, Loreal Kids, and Ozark Spring Water for Kids to Colgate Spongebob SquarePants, TicTalk cell phones, and Sports Illustrated Kids (with a special web site, www.sikids.com). The new fashion craze is branded clothes lines just for kids, such as Gap Kids, Eddie Bauer Kids, and now even Sheen Kidz and Kidtoure t-shirts.

Plainly, not all teens have shared equally in the recent prosperity, nor in the commercial obsession with children that has accompanied it. In 2000, child poverty rates reached record lows, but since then have begun inching back up. Even in 2005, however, poverty rates for every racial and ethnic group remain much lower today than in any year before 1999. Millennials in the bottom quarter of the household income distribution are, in absolute terms (size of home, plumbing, air-conditioning, personal bedrooms, toys, vaccinations, family ownership of car, and so on), much better off than they were in the '80s or '60s.

Several categories of goods and services—from phones to consumer electronics to restaurant meals—are less expensive for Millennials, in inflation-adjusted dollars, than they were for their Boomer parents in youth. The falling relative price of processed and fast foods is a contributing factor to the recent rise in youth obesity, which has been especially dramatic among lower-income and immigrant families. Yet as some items have become less expensive, other products and services fundamental to life—in particular, health care, home ownership, and higher education—are substantially more costly now for young people than they were one or two generations ago.

For some groups, the sense of relative economic deprivation may be as acute as ever. Kids from low-income families are more likely to compare themselves to affluent kids, and affluent kids to hyper-wealthy kids (whose lifestyle is the focus of so much media attention). Middle-income kids—especially collegians—feel especially vulnerable in an era when the idea of a comfortable middle class is being eroded by luxury on one side and deprivation on the other. Low-income African-American youths face an extra burden. The spectacular and highly visible success of extremely wealthy sports and entertainment stars tends to undermine the morale of kids who are striving hard to plan and qualify for other careers.

The Parent-Child Co-purchase

Most of the Millennial spending boom has been fueled by parental money, not Millennials' own. Over the past fifteen years, the types of kid income that have risen the most are the types that parents most firmly manage (gifts, joint purchases, and paid household work). The types that have risen the least—or even declined—are the types that parents least control ("weekly allowances" and paid employment). Both trends defy the free-agent "proto-adult" youth stereotype of the Gen-X youth era.

The fastest-growing source of teen cash has been the direct ad-hoc payment from parent to child, often for a specific purchase on which parent and child confer. Since such payments are neither child spending nor parent spending, these consensual transactions resist the categories favored by many marketing experts. One teen in three now says ad-hoc cash from parents is his or her biggest source of income. Supplementing parental payments are gifts from grandparents, 55 percent of whom say they've given their grandkids one or more gifts in the prior month.

Another rapidly growing teen cash source is income earned through household chores, which often mingles with the parental "gift" category. During the Millennial child era, more parents have been working longer hours—too long, in the eyes of many Millennials, who look forward to leading more balanced lives. Millennials have adapted to such workaholic households by spending substantially more time than Gen Xers did on tasks previously performed by parents, from food shopping to cooking to laundry to caring for siblings. And they're being paid for it. From 1991 to 1997, money from teen chores more than doubled.

Other income sources are falling in importance, including "allowances" unrelated to specific tasks. To many a Boomer and Gen-X parent, each dollar in "allowance money" seems wasted when that same dollar might be used to reward, instruct, punish, cajole, or moralize. Teen income from paid employment outside the home is also falling, reflecting the view of teens and parents that other uses of time (like being on a school basketball team or interning for city hall) could be more influential to college admissions committees.

For all of these reasons, teens are buying more things jointly with their parents. Teens ask parents for money to buy something, they together discuss whether it's a worthwhile purchase, the parents hand out the money, and teens go to the store (or on-line) to make the purchase. Officials at the Center for a New American Dream have noted a new "nag factor" driving many youth purchases, with ten percent of 12- and 13-year-olds saying they ask their parents more than fifty times for products they've seen advertised.

While parents are often paying in full for major teen purchases (like expensive tickets to rock concerts) that in times past were more financed by youth work and savings, parents also appear to be influencing lesser teen purchases through rules, advice, and earmarked cash. At the same time, teens are influencing parental purchase decisions on big-ticket items like cars, houses, and vacations (by voicing their opinion), and on small-ticket items like groceries and take-out food (by saving their parents' time).

Thus has emerged the era of the parent-teen "co-purchase."

Twenty years ago, the big new trend in youth marketing was the independent child purchase. Today, the new trend is the child purchasing only after receiving a parent's approval, alias the co-purchase. The corollary of this is the "co-target," where marketers treat the child and parent as influencers of each other's purchases, from a teen's school clothes to mom's new car. To close the sale, you have to market to both parties.

Millennial teens frequently consult with parents on buying decisions. "Today's working parents feel so guilty about not spending time with their children that they try to compensate by offering them more consumer power," *The Financial Times* reported in 1997. "Others believe today's child-rearing practices fit in with Baby Boomers' respect for individual desires. And others say children's participation in purchasing decisions reflects, in part, parents' uncertainty about high-technology items."

The co-purchase is a new Millennial-era phenomenon. In the early '80s, Nickelodeon successfully promoted itself to Gen-X 'tweens as a "parent-free zone." A decade later, when the focus-group reaction was no longer favorable, Nick dropped the slogan.

Big Brands Are Back

In teen purchasing power and youth market trends, a new generational universe is emerging. Millennials are beginning to reconnect the youth and adult markets and to reunite the splintered and narrowcast buying habits inherited from Gen X. They are transforming the commercial role of youth through positive peer pressure, cooperative choice-making with parents, and easily accessible new teen media. With Instant Messenger, chat rooms, e-stores, and social software arenas like MySpace, they are the first youth generation in which virtually any member can keep up hour-to-hour with the opinions and tastes of peers across the nation.

Niche markets are foundering. Big brands are back. Aided by new technologies, from web chat to cell phones, Millennials pay keen attention to what's happening at the gravitational center of their peer group, whether on-line at one of the new multi-user game sites, or in person at Target and Wal-Mart (both of which enjoyed post-9/11 boosts in teen buying). Mass fads, big brands, group focus, and a lower-profile commercial style are ready for a come-back. Meanwhile, "the edge" has peaked—along with weak product loyalties, hyper-commercialism, and the focus on risk and self.

Mass marketers have taken full note of this. In the April 1998 issue of *American Demographics*, Texas A&M professor James McNeal foresaw that "advertising that encourages children to defy their parents, make fun of author-ity, or talk unintelligibly will be replaced with informative ads describing the benefits of products." That was nearly a decade ago, and the "informed" chil-dren of the early '90s are now the undergrads on campus. Marketers have found them a difficult group to reach—in part because the "edge" no longer works as well. Calvin Klein and Abercrombie & Fitch, faced with softening demand for their labels, have recently retooled, replacing the ultra-edgy "in your face" approach that worked so well in the '90s with a friendlier attitude clearly aimed at Millennials. Television ads (and celebrity endorsements) are weakening as youth influencers, while peers and parents are rising in importance.

Whatever you're selling, whether soap, cars, or colleges, the way to connect with Millennials is to brand your image, target the mainstream, wrap yourself around positive youth values, and make room for the family in your message.

Organization Kids

During their 'tween and teen years, the experience of working for money out-side the home has not been as common for Millennials as it was for previous generations. This is a measure of the extra sheltering and structure in their lives. By the time they become college students in their twenties, on the other hand, Millennials are going to work somewhat more than previous generations. This is a measure of the extra cost of college today—and of the pressure they feel to make ends meet.

Year to year, teen employment usually tracks the patterns of adult employ-ment. In a recession, when one peaks, the other does at about the same time. Yet over the longer term, teen employment often does not track the employment of older age brackets. For example, you would think the stagflationary '70s would have been a shakeout time for teen workers, and the roaring '90s a growth time. But very much the opposite occurred. From one generation to the next, shifting parental and youth attitudes have played key roles in pushing teen employment up or down. Teen employment was low for the Silent, rising for Boomers, and high for Gen Xers—and now, for Millennials, falling again.

For Boomer teens, the "right" to work was a newly won youth freedom. Then Gen Xers came along and pushed teen workloads higher. Summer and after-school teen work grew strongly and almost continuously from the mid-'60s to the early '80s, when late-wave Boomers and first-wave Gen Xers (girls especially) pushed paid teen employment to a postwar peak. Xers kept it near these high levels for the rest of the decade.

Throughout the Gen-X youth era, the purpose of teen work was shifting away from supporting families and toward personal spending money, career-building, or self-fulfillment. One of every six 15-year-olds held an after-school job, one of every three a paid summer job, and, for the first time ever, employed girls outnumbered employed boys. Later in the '80s, as adult immigrants began moving into the service sector, teen employment began to ebb slightly. By the late '80s, employment rates for 16- and 17-year-olds were roughly 5 percent below those of the late '70s. Rates for 15-year-olds were 20 percent lower.

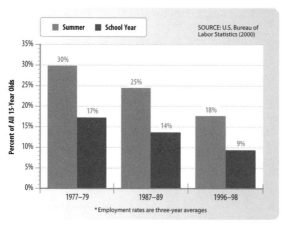

Figure 16 ▶

Employment Rate of 15-Year-Olds, Late '70s to Late '90s

In the Millennial youth era, employment has continued to fall among teens, especially younger teens, despite an economy that, through the year 2000, desperately wanted young workers and was willing to pay plenty for them. Then came another recession and 9/11. Whereas the share of employed teens age 16 to 19 drifted down from 47 percent in 1979 to 44 percent in 2000, by 2005 it had plunged all the way to 36 percent (the lowest rate ever recorded since records were first kept in 1948), with virtually no recovery since then.

What accounts for the ebbing popularity of paid work for teenagers? One reason, accounting for about half of the decline, is that teens are spending more time in grade school (longer days and more summer school). Another reason is that attitudes have changed. During the '90s, educators, parents, and teens themselves began to have second thoughts about whether too many teens were wrapping tacos when they ought to be wrestling with math. Families looked around and began noticing what would pay off for their children. Young adults (aged 25 to 34) with four-year college degrees were the only young adults whose full-time earnings have been beating inflation. When the bottom line is getting into a good college, time spent on computer lessons, select soccer, community service, or SAT prep courses seems more valuable, long-term, than time spent on mere money making. As a result, many of the service jobs Gen-X teens once held are now held, not by Millennial teens, but by older Gen-X immigrants.

By the time Millennials become adults, this aversion to paid work apparently disappears. Adjusted for the business cycle, the employment rate of youths age 20 to 24 has been basically flat over the past twenty-five years, with no downward trend after 2000. Among college students, employment was actually higher in 2003 (a very weak year for the economy) than it was in 1979. Clearly, many Millennial collegians who never worked in grade school are now urgently seeking employment in college, either to help cover the high cost of tuition, to ease the burden on parents, or to pay for their living expenses. Some administrators complain that these collegiate workers lack the "soft skills" (punctuality, politeness, proper dress, and so on) that earlier youth generations learned

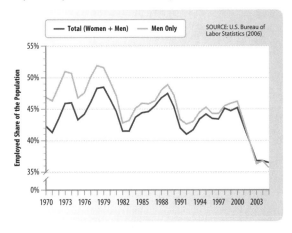

◄ **Figure 17**

Employment Rates for Youth Age 16 to 19, 1970 to 2005

on the job at an earlier age. Others suggest, more constructively, that colleges make "workplace training" a required course for the entire student body.

Millennials have been entering the full-time workforce with high school degrees since 2000 and with four-year college degrees since 2004. Already, businesses are beginning to take stock of the opportunities and challenges this generation presents. On the plus side, employers report that they excel in group work, crave approval, are very teachable, like to plan their futures, and take a genuine interest in the overall purpose of the organization. On the negative side, employers report that they require a lot of oversight, avoid creative risks, are unfamiliar with the bottom-line demands of paid employment, and are overly attached to their parents and families. Few employers would have reported these traits when talking about Generation X (or Boomers) at the same entry-level age.

The Price of Higher Education

With application numbers surging, busy admissions directors understand that the share of high schools graduates trying to get into college has never been so large. With huge bills to pay, sticker-shocked freshmen and their parents are equally aware that the price of entry continues to get steeper.

Few college leaders have taken a public position on the sustainability or consequences of the seemingly endless escalation of tuitions over the last quarter-century. Most simply point to their costs and figure that if parents can still pay it, they can still charge it. This may be a mistake. No price can indefinitely rise faster than family income—not for stocks, not for houses, and not for colleges. If the bubble bursts, vulnerable colleges with no contingency plan may find themselves in trouble. And even if the rising trend does not break soon, or breaks only gradually, colleges that understand and respond to the growing role of price in shaping the perceptions of Millennials and their parents will be at a large advantage in the years to come.

Back when the Boomer parents of today's collegians were themselves in college, price was not a big problem. In 1965—in dollars inflation-adjusted to 2006—tuition and fees averaged just under $7,000 for a four-year private college and just under $2,000 for an equivalent public college. Over the next fifteen years, the prices didn't change much in real terms, drifting up a bit for private schools and down a bit for public schools. In an era when the real median household income grew from around $35,000 to $40,000, this was a very affordable deal—and not just for the median family. Because incomes were more tightly packed around a "middle class," four-fifths of all households had incomes greater than twice the average private college tuition.

The surging tide of Boomer teens who wanted higher education during the '60s ratcheted up the demand-side pressure, but older generations kept tuitions down by expanding supply. They built new facilities and hired new faculty. Voters in many states agreed to higher taxes in order to fund enormous expansions in public university systems, which then accepted resident freshmen for practically no tuition at all. In 1965, Congress passed the Higher Education Act, which mandated need-based grants, subsidized loans, and work-study programs for hard-up students. Millions of middle-class Boomers worked their way through four-year colleges while borrowing very little. Those who preceded Boomers—the Silent Generation, many of whom are now trustees or overseers of colleges and universities—nearly always completed their educations completely debt-free.

Starting in the early 1980s, just as the first Gen Xers entered college as freshmen, this arrangement began to fall apart. That was when tuitions began to rise faster than inflation year after year.

A new mood hit America that reassured every institution, including those in higher education, that it was now acceptable to seek profitability and respond to market signals. Many colleges figured they could push families closer to the brink of affordability—and use the proceeds to enhance their quality and competitive reputation. Ambitious Gen-X college applicants and their parents took a hard look at the erosion of the non-college middle class and gladly paid up. An expensive degree seemed a small price to pay for being able to jump to the upper end of life's income distribution. The public sector, meanwhile, did little or nothing to restrain tuition hikes by encouraging alternative credentialing paths or by expanding the capacity of four-year state colleges, many of which suffered budget cuts in the '90s and needed to raise tuitions to make ends meet.

A familiar refrain during the Gen-X college era was that the "college earnings premium" made college a bargain at any price. As Millennials reached campuses in 2000, a new catchword—"globalization"—summed up family fears that without a brand-name degree their kids would be fated to compete against low-wage foreign workers for the rest of their lives.

The end result? From 1980 to 2006, on average, private four-year tuitions rose 4.0 percent faster than inflation *every year*. Public four-year tuitions rose even faster (about 4.5 percent above inflation annually). By 2006, the average private four-year tuition had grown to $22,218, and the average public four-year tuition to $5,836—in both cases around three times higher in real dollars than they were back in 1965. Over the same period, the real income of the median household only rose by 30 percent. Today, only half of all households earn more than double the average four-year tuition for a private college, down sharply from the 1960s.

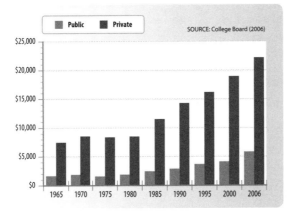

Figure 18 ▶

Average Yearly Tuition and Fees at Four-Year Colleges, in Constant 2006 Dollars

The price of higher education includes a number of additional factors. On top of tuition, most students need to pay rent—which has recently been soaring in most campus towns. Textbook prices have risen so rapidly that they are now the target of a federal inquiry. Add in the total extra cost of room, board, and expenses, and the average cost of a four-year private college in 2006 rises to just over $30,000. Subtract all the grants-in-aid that students receive, on the other hand, and the average drops back to around $21,000. Though grants per student have risen as fast as the tuition list price over the last decade, even the "net" price of college continues to outpace prices and incomes by a substantial margin. What's worse, little of the increase in grants has been flowing toward low-income students. Instead, both private and state colleges nowadays use a rising share of their grants to lure attractive students away from competitors—a practice known as "discounting."

Let's take these two trends—tuitions rising much faster than the median income and a declining share of grants targeting the poor—and combine them with a third: the widening distribution of family incomes around the median during the '80s and '90s, with high-income families gaining much faster than inflation and low-income families falling behind. The outcome is marginal discomfort at the high end but an affordability crisis at the low end, as confirmed by the College Board in its 2005 *Trends in College Pricing* report. From 1993 to 2004, the cost of attending a private four-year college (net of grants) grew only slightly, from 17 to 19 percent of family income, for the top quarter of all families. But the cost grew dramatically, from 60 to 83 percent of family income, for the bottom quarter.

Compounding the sheer affordability burden is the growing need to borrow to bridge the family resource gap. Federal student lending per student has grown as fast as tuitions over the past twenty-five years, though the pace since 2000 appears to be slowing a bit. Total federal lending to students, now at $69 billion per year, has doubled over the past decade. Private college lenders, almost unheard of in 1990, are now underwriting an additional $14 billion per year.

As of the 2003–04 academic year, 73 percent of graduates from four-year private college have taken out an average of $24,600 in student loans. The figures for four-year state colleges are 62 percent and $15,500, respectively. These are just undergraduate averages, and don't include the large numbers of Millennials leaving college with debts of over $50,000 or those now entering medical or law school, who can expect to graduate with debts of well over $100,000. Even these numbers do not include the extra credit-card debt racked up by an estimated quarter of all students to help pay tuition and fees. Or the extra home-equity loans or 401(k) loans taken out by parents, most of them Boomers, many of whom are trying to save for their own retirement. According to the Chartwells 2006 College Student Survey, 41 percent of Millennial undergrads say that paying for college will be a "very" or "extremely" difficult financial burden. Fifty-one percent say their college debt will affect their career choices.

Thus far, the challenge of rising college prices is affecting Millennials in ways characteristic of their generation. It is adding to the pressure they feel about the future and the need to plan ahead, such as figuring out how to repay large student loans on entry-level salaries. It is bringing them even closer to their families, to the extent that most college youth hardly bother to distinguish anymore between their own housing and financial resources and those of their parents. It is further sensitizing them to the widening class and income gaps within their generation, fissures that threaten their hopes for a more cohesive national community. Tuitions and student borrowing grew far more during the Gen-X student era than they have in recent years, but Gen Xers did not often respond in these ways.

Nor did the cost of college cause such public alarm. That is something else very Millennial about the college price problem: Like every other trend that is deemed to be threatening to this generation's future, it won't be allowed to continue. The media glare will grow harsher. The statements from public officials will grow more critical. Most importantly, parents will begin demanding that colleges re-examine their entire product from a price- and value-oriented perspective—a demand that will be catalyzed by the arrival of the Gen-X parent on campus. We will rejoin this prediction in Part Three (on page161), where we discuss how most colleges can best go about retooling and re-pricing their product for the next decade.

5 | Seven Core Traits

"The Millennials, the first batch of which
are the high school class of 2000, …are,
as a group, pleasant, cheerful, helpful,
ambitious, and community-oriented."

— MARY ANN JOHNSON, FILM CRITIC (2000)

Seven Core Traits

Every generation contains all kinds of people. But each generation has a persona, with core traits. Not all members of that generation will share those traits, and many will personally resist those traits, but—like it or not—those core traits will substantially define the world inhabited by every member of a generation.

The following are the seven core traits of the Millennial Generation.

* **Special.** From precious-baby movies of the mid-'80s to the media glare surrounding the high school Class of 2000, older generations have inculcated in Millennials the sense that they are, collectively, vital to the nation and to their parents' sense of purpose.

* **Sheltered.** From the surge in child-safety rules and devices to the post-Columbine lockdown of public schools to the hotel-style security of today's college dorm rooms, Millennials have been the focus of the most sweeping youth-protection movement in American history.

* **Confident.** With high levels of trust and optimism—and a newly felt connection to parents and future—Millennials are equating good news for themselves with good news for their country.

* **Team-Oriented.** From Barney and team sports to collaborative learning and community service, Millennials have developed strong team instincts and tight peer bonds.

* **Conventional.** Taking pride in their improving behavior and comfortable with their parents' values, Millennials provide a modern twist to the traditional belief that social rules and standards can make life easier.

* **Pressured.** Pushed to study hard, avoid personal risks, and take full advantage of the collective opportunities adults are offering them, Millennials feel a "trophy kid" pressure to excel.
* **Achieving.** As accountability and higher school standards have risen to the top of America's political agenda, Millennials have become a generation focused on achievement—and are on track to becoming the smartest, best-educated young adults in U.S. history.

On the whole, these are not traits one would have associated with Silent, Boomers, or Gen Xers, in youth, but they are traits remembered from the days of G.I. Generation teens.

Millennials and Specialness

Millennials first arrived in the early '80s as the offspring of "yuppie" parents touting "family values"—of Boomer supermoms opting to have in vitro babies (a historical first) and Boomer dads demanding to be to be present at childbirth (another historical first). When this first Millennial wave entered grade school in 1989, America suddenly mobilized around a national school reform movement. A few years later, with the end of the Cold War, the fate of children became the central focus of political speeches, new legislation, and a gathering culture war. By 1998, more than half of all Americans (a record share) said that "getting kids off to the right start" ought to be America's top priority. National issues having nothing directly to do with children—Social Security, the War on Terror, unemployment—began to be discussed in terms of their impact on children.

As Millennials have absorbed the adult message that they dominate America's agenda, they have come easily to the belief that *their* problems are the *nation's* problems, *their* future is the *nation's* future, and, by extension, everyone in America will naturally be inclined to help them solve those problems.

When asked which groups will be most likely to help America toward a better future, teens rank "young people" second, behind only "scientists." When asked whose generation can have the greatest impact on what the global environment will become twenty-five years from now, 86 percent say their own, and only 9 percent say their parents'. When asked the same question, their parents mostly agree, 71 percent saying their children's generation will have the most impact. When asked which of today's living generations has the highest reputation and which they would most like to emulate, Millennial high school seniors (by lopsided majorities) say their grandparents' generation—the can-do, war-winning, "greatest generation."

Even as Millennials leave home for college, their parents find it hard to let these special kids go. On campuses, administrators are expanding their "empty nest" orientation programs for doting moms and dads, complete with teddy bears for them to hug. With catchy titles like, "What Have You Done with My Child?" (University of North Carolina at Wilmington) and "May They Follow Your Path, and Not Your Footsteps" (Ohio Northern University), they are designed to assure audiences that the colleges are merely adding the final touches on their wonderful progeny. According to the Datatel 2006 College Parent Survey, today's parents spend much more time with their college-aged kids than their own parents did with them. By a three-to-one margin, today's parents say they are more involved in helping their children succeed in college.

After graduation, Millennials and their parents often want to stay close. Since 2004, according to the MonsterTRAK annual on-line survey, roughly 60 percent of college grads say they plan to move back in with their parents, at least temporarily. One-quarter of Boomers say they expect their children or grandchildren to live with them at some point during retirement—and Millennial teens are now more likely than Gen-X teens were to say they would like to live and work near their parents. Over the past quarter-century, the attitude of every age bracket toward multigenerational households has become more favorable. In 1973, only 33 percent of young adults felt it was a good idea for older people to share a home with grown children, and 56 percent felt it was a bad idea. By 1994, those proportions had reversed, to 55 percent thinking it good and 28 percent thinking it bad.

The new popularity of extended family households has coincided with a growth in the size (and cost) of an average family home. For reasons of lifestyle, cultural tastes, and simple economics, it today makes far more sense for young adults to share homes with their parents than it did when Boomers were young. Once common, then frowned upon by young and old alike as the first three generations came of age after World War II, the extended family is again becoming a new norm in Twenty-First Century America.

Millennials and Sheltering

Americans have been tightening the security perimeters around Millennials ever since this generation began arriving over twenty years ago. Adults have gradually pulled down per-capita rates of divorce, abortion, alcohol consumption, and other dangers to children. As worried parents, they've become avid consumers for a child-proofing industry that has snapped up new patents for everything from stove-knob covers to safety mirrors. This new sheltering trend has reversed the trends that today's older generations recall from their own youth eras, when adult protectiveness was being dismantled (for Boomers) or not really there at all (for Gen Xers). In the Datetel College Parent Survey, a large majority of parents say that they have worked harder to protect their kids from harm than their own parents did with them. This majority is larger for younger Gen-X parents than for older Boomer parents.

Millennials look up at a castle-like edifice of parental care that keeps getting new bricks added—"smart lockers" and carding at the movies last month, graduated licenses and bedroom spy cams this month, children's car-helmets next month. The Internet remains a refuge of youth freedom, to some degree, but the software designers are constructing new protective boundaries there too. The older '80s-born Millennials recall a world with more open sky, while the younger ones born in the '90s look up at the growing walls, unable to imagine what could be seen in their absence.

Since 9/11, the protective boundaries have drawn even closer—with national TV coverage of "amber alert" warnings for missing children and the marketing of "home security" devices that allow parents to track their kids via GPS. Parents can now monitor their children's movements with "SmartWear" tags sewn into their clothing, and monitoring devices for cars (that can alert the parent by email if a young person exceeds the speed limit or drives beyond a predefined boundary). When Millennials entered college, administrators began reporting a huge increase in "helicopter parents" who constantly phone and email faculty and deans to talk about grades, moods, foods, or whatever, in the belief that their children require extra care.

Younger Millennials in middle school may be even more supportive of extra protection than the older ones now in high school or college. Seven years ago, in the first months after Columbine, older teens wanted to increase rather than decrease school security by a two-to-one margin, while younger teens said the same by a four-to-one margin. When sweeping new rules such as metal detectors or student identity cards have been proposed in K-12 schools, the usual experience is initial student resistance, but only until those measures are put in place, after which many students change their minds and become supportive. By huge majorities, Millennial teens support harsh punishments (including expulsion) for those who misbehave.

All of this sheltering has created a youth generation that is, on the whole, much healthier and less prone to injury and predation than any earlier generation in American history. Infant mortality and death rates from disease, violence, and accidents are all down by at least a third from what they were at the same age for Gen Xers. Thanks in part to more aggressive law enforcement and social service intervention, federal data show that, between 1988 and 1999, rates of child abduction fell by 23 percent, runaways by 25 percent, substantiated child abuse by 43 percent, and missing children by 51 percent.

Yet the urge to shelter has also been responsible for some new health problems among Millennials. Consider, for example, the dramatic decline in their physical activity—especially unstructured activity outdoors. In 1969, half of all 18-year-olds walked or rode a bike to school. Today, hardly any teens do that, making kids six times more likely to play a video game than ride a bike on a typical day. Just since 1995, bike riding is down by one-third—as is the share of children ages 7 to 11 who swim, fish, canoe, or play touch football. Since 1997, baseball playing is down 28 percent. Meanwhile, physical education classes at schools are being cut back to make room for more academics. Most experts agree that this decline in physical activity has contributed to the quadrupling (from 4 to 16 percent) in the share of children and teens classified by the Centers for Disease Control and Prevention as "pre-obese"—and perhaps also to the rising incidence of ADD and ADHD. Increasing body mass indices (along with a new emphasis on cleanliness) may also be pushing the rising incidence of asthma among kids.

True to the wishes of adult America, Millennials are protected, feel protected, and expect to be protected—even, some might say, overprotected.

Millennials and Confidence

In May 1997, Canadian journalist Deborah Jones dubbed Millennials the "Sunshine Generation," recognizing that, on both sides of the border, 'tweens and teens comprised the happiest age bracket. For over thirty years, until the mid-'90s, the teen suicide rate marched relentlessly upward. Over the last decade, it has declined by a third. Where polls show adults believing that being a parent is getting harder, they show Millennials believing that being a kid has gotten easier. In 1994, 70 percent of (Gen-X) 13- to 17-year-olds said it's "harder" to grow up now than in their parents' time. By 1999, among Millennials, that percentage had dropped to 43 percent. In 2005, 67 percent of 15 to 22 year olds rated themselves as happy or very happy most of the time.

"Why are kids so confident?" asked a recent KidsPeace report. "Significantly, the word 'crisis' seems not to appear in the teen lexicon." The Cold War is over. The War on Terror is winnable. And even if the economy grows in fits and starts and the federal budget is deep in the red, well, the Internet keeps getting faster and cell phones cheaper. Like their cartoon hero Spongebob SquarePants, Millennials believe that the irrepressible optimist can overcome all obstacles.

Two years after 9/11, with the economy still struggling to recover, more than half of all teens agreed that "people my age should be optimistic about their chances of having a good job." Among those in families earning less than $30,000, 54 percent believed the world holds "many opportunities for me." Among those in families earning over $75,000, that proportion rose to 78 percent. By 2005, 65 percent of youths age 18 to 25—including 75 percent of young Blacks and Latinos—predicted they would be "financially better off than their parents."

The teen view of success has become better rounded and less exclusively focused on one life goal. Over the last decade, "marriage/family" and "career success" have each declined in importance as "the one thing" in life. What's

Freshman Attitudes, Then and Now

	Year (%)			
	1974	1983	1990	2006
Objectives considered essential or very important				
Raising a family	55	66	70	76
Developing a meaningful philosophy of life	61	44	43	46
Being very well-off financially	44	69	72	73
Agree strongly or somewhat				
Marijuana should be legalized	47	26	19	37
Abortion should be legal	n/a	55	65	57
It is important to have laws prohibiting homosexual relationships	n/a	49	44	26
Sex is ok even if two people know little about each other	46	49	51	45[a]
Realistically, an individual can do little to bring about changes in society	44	37	31	27

[a] For 2005
SOURCE: The American Freshman, UCLA, 1998–2006

become far more important is the concept of *balance*—between learning and play, academic life and social life, and, down the road, between work life and family life. A rising share of high school seniors say "making a contribution to society" is "extremely" or "quite" important, while a declining share (though still a majority) say the same for "having lots of money." As the first Millennials enter the workplace, recent surveys have shown that "lead a balanced life" has risen in importance as a personal goal.

In a turnabout from Gen-X youths of the '80s, Millennials have faith that the American Dream will work not only for them but for their own children. Sixty-nine percent say they're more optimistic than pessimistic about the world their children will live in, while only 24 percent say they're more pessimistic. These teens see the future with a far longer view than their parents did at the same age. The share who defines success as "being able to give my children better opportunities than I had" has reached an all-time high.

The events of 9/11 and the prospect of related economic shocks have shaken the confidence of many Millennials, but much less so than older Americans. Of all age groups, Millennials have proved to be the least perturbed by the new security measures, including violations of civil rights and intrusions against privacy. The first several Millennial cohorts had their own 9/11, more than three years earlier, in April of 1999, at Columbine High School in Littleton, Colorado. In the remaining six weeks of that traumatic school year, middle and high school students learned what would happen if they kept sharp objects in their pockets, played with a toy gun, or cracked jokes about student shooters. Come 9/11, they were already familiar with scanners, cameras, metal detectors, see-through backpacks, and unlockable lockers. These first Millennial cohorts then set the tone for those born in the late 1980s or '90s, who tend to accept security measures without question or complaint.

More than older people, Millennials have grown accustomed to the sight of aggressive security. And more than older generations, they tend to associate such shows of force with safety (rather than with threats to liberty). In this sense, teenage Millennials appear to be better prepared, functionally and emotionally, for the new mood of post-9/11 America.

Millennials and Team-Orientation

Surrounded by individualistic older people, yet optimistic about their own abilities and prospects, Millennials have stepped into a Gen-X-styled youth world that, in their view, lacks cohesion. They're now busy trying to make all the pieces fit together better.

The team ethic shows up in a new youth aversion to disorder within their own social setting—starting with classrooms. When public school students are asked what most needs fixing in their schools, most of them mention teaching "good manners," "maintaining discipline in the classroom," and making students "treat each other with respect." Forty percent want something to be done about unruly student behavior that interferes with schoolwork. Back in the Gen-X youth era, educators disliked peer pressure because they associated the concept with rule-breaking. Today, educators are discovering that peer pressure can be harnessed to better enforce rules—through group projects, peer grading, student juries, and the like.

The new team orientation has broadened Millennials' search for peer friendships, drawing them to circles and cliques. Only three teens in ten report that they usually socialize with only one or two friends, while two in three do so with groups of friends. The proportion of eighth- and tenth-graders who felt lonely or wish they had more friends declined sharply from 1991 to 1998. A rising share would prefer to stay with their friends after graduation. Teachers report that, compared with students of a decade ago, those of today feel closer to each other.

This Millennial cliquishness has made peer pressure a much bigger teen issue than before, yet Millennials see it more positively than adults do. Many see peers as a source of help, comfort, and power. Only about one-third of teens say they are under "some" or "a great deal" of pressure from peers to "break rules," although a larger share report being teased about clothing, and bullying (especially verbal aggression among girls) is reported to be a rising problem.

Millennial teens and collegians are adapting new cell phone, networking, and social software technologies (like MySpace and Facebook) to increase their level of interconnection to a level that has never been seen in any prior generation. They're less interested in the anonymous freedom of the Internet and more interested in its ability to maintain peer networks. Roughly one-half (thirty-four million) of all u.s. kids under age 18 were on-line in 2003, comprising one-fifth of all u.s. Internet users. Of those on-line, nearly all use Instant Messaging (IM) services to talk to friends. A typical Millennial can have one or two hundred "buddies" on her IM list. As internet-based computer games become less violent and more interactive, more Millennial players are signing on.

The team ethic even shows up in the new political views of youth. In the 2006 UCLA American Freshmen Survey, 67 percent of Millennial teens said it is essential or very important to help others who are in difficulty, the highest response in twenty-six years. Other surveys have shown that when teens are asked to identify "the major causes" of America's problems, their seven most popular answers all pertain to what they perceive as an excess of adult individualism. Reason number one (given by 56 percent of all teens) is "selfishness, people not thinking of the rights of others." Reason number two (given by 52 percent) is "people who don't respect the law and the authorities." Meanwhile, "lack of parental discipline of children and teens"—an answer very few Boomer teens would ever have given—ranks as reason number four.

In college, Millennials are voting and participating in political activities much more energetically than Gen-X students did through the 1980s and '90s. In 2005, the share of college freshmen reporting that they worked in a political campaign in the previous year was the highest since 1971. In the 2004 presidential election, the voter turnout rate among people ages 18 to 24 increased by 11 points, from 36 to 47 percent, while the overall electorate showed only a 4 percent increase. Youth participation rose even more strikingly in the states where pre-election polls had shown the outcome to be in doubt. As the first cohorts of Millennials reach voting age, they are quickly closing the gap in voter turnout between voters in their early twenties (age 18 to 24) and late-wave Xer voters who are roughly ten years older (age 25 to 34). This gap is now the smallest since the U.S. Census first undertook national age-based voter surveys in 1964.

Unlike Boomers, more Millennials would like to rescue the "establishment" than attack it. The Boomer rebellion was energized by surging advocacy under the banners of feminism and racial and ethnic empowerment, aimed at a powerful and complacent middle class full of Archie Bunkers. For the Boomers' children, these issues no longer carry the same voltage. Millennials are more concerned that rising economic inequality is weakening America's middle class, which today feels, on the whole, neither powerful nor complacent.

The distribution of income and wealth has changed markedly over two generations. When Boomers were young, the differences in pay, housing, and buying patterns across the economic spectrum—from manual laborers to teachers to lawyers to movies stars and pro athletes—were relatively narrow. In the 1960s, a corporate CEO earned about thirty times (and an athlete about four times) more than what a schoolteacher did. Now, in the new century, those numbers are three hundred times (and twenty times) more, respectively. While there are some young people for whom family money is freely available—who get substantial help from parents for everything from buying cars and houses to starting careers and launching businesses—there are a much larger number who do not have these advantages.

Given this generation's powerful team instincts, many young people find these circumstances troubling. The Millennial response to income and wealth inequality will likely shape their personal and political agendas, with major, long-term effects on America's cultural and civic life—just as these trends are today affecting life on campus.

Millennials and Convention

Boomer children felt overdosed on norms and rules, and famously came of age assaulting them. Millennials show signs of trying to re-establish a regime of rules. Where Boomer teens commonly had trouble talking to their parents—a major cause of the late-'60s "generation gap"—Millennials have far less trouble doing so. Their rebellion lies in moving to the ordered center, rather than pushing the anarchic edge.

Why this Millennial move to the center? Having benefited from a re-norming of family life following the turbulent 1960s and 1970s, today's teens are inclined to feel trust in the core aspects of their daily lives. Compared to Gen Xers, Millennials bask in the sense of being loved by parents. In 1995, 93 percent of 10- to 13-year-olds (who today are 21- to 24-year-olds) felt "loved" all or almost all the time. In a 1997 Gallup survey, nine in ten youths reported being very close to their parents and personally happy—much closer than twenty years earlier.

In fact, Millennials describe closer ties with their parents than any teens in the history of postwar polling. Earlier this decade, two-thirds of teenagers said that their parents were "in touch" with their lives, and six in ten said it was "easy" to talk with parents about sex, drugs, and alcohol. In a 1998 teen survey, 80 percent reported having had "really important talks" with their parents, and 94 percent mostly or totally agreed that "I can always trust my parents to be there when I need them." Back in 1974, more than 40 percent of Boomers flatly declared they'd "be better off not living with their parents." Many parents now report that their Millennial children tell them everything about their lives, far beyond what Boomers ever dared tell their own moms and dads. The special relationship between Millennials and their parents is reflected everywhere in today's culture—even in a popular new line of Hallmark greeting cards that reads "to my mother, my best friend."

Far more than anything Boomers or Gen Xers can remember, today's teens and parents share tastes in clothes, music, and other entertainments. Revivals of Boomer-era music classics can be Millennial hits, and teens think nothing of introducing their parents to the latest music download. Part of what has made "American Idol" so successful has been how Millennials and their parents have rooted together for shared favorites. Behind this trend lies a deeper agreement on underlying cultural values. The share of teens reporting "very different" values from their parents has fallen by roughly half since the '70s, and the share who say their values are "very or mostly similar" has hit an all-time high of 76 percent

While Millennials are broadly willing to accept their parents' exacting values (and spacious homes), they are also starting to think they can apply these values, and someday run the show, a whole lot better. When asked whether "values and character" will matter more or less to their own generation when they're parents, they answer "more" by a two-to-one margin. Today's young people are far more trusting than their parents of the capacity of large national institutions to do the right thing for their generation and for the country. When teens are asked who's going to improve the schools, clean up the environment, and cut the crime rate, they respond—without irony—that it will be teachers, government, and police. Among college students, careers in government are highly regarded.

"One of the macro-trends we're seeing is neo-traditionalism," says teen-marketer Kirsty Doig. "These kids are fed up with the superficialities of life. They have not had a lot of stability in their lives. It's a backlash, a return to tradition and ritual." This doesn't mean Millennials are a generation of conservative throwbacks—their tolerant views on gay rights and their trust in big government set them far apart from most older conservatives. They are, rather, a generation that seeks norms and structure and a return to civic life—with an underlying sense that rules and standards can often make life easier.

Older people are sometimes blindsided by the new traditionalism (or at what some less accurately call the "new conservatism") of today's teens. Few would guess that the share of college freshmen who say raising a family is an "important" life goal rose to 75 percent in 2003—up from only 59 percent in 1977. Even parents are sometimes surprised. Nearly half of Boomers, when interviewed, believe it must be embarrassing for teens to admit they are virgins, yet only a quarter of teens themselves agree. The burgeoning "youth chastity" subculture has recently attracted much incredulous coverage from media with older readerships—for example, a 2005 *Rolling Stone* feature, entitled "The New Virgin Army: Life Among the Young and Sexless."

Earlier this decade, George Gallup, Jr. summed up the evidence as follows: "Teens today are decidedly more traditional than their elders were, in both lifestyles and attitudes. Gallup Youth Survey data from the past twenty-five years reveal that teens today are far less likely than their parents were to use alcohol, tobacco and marijuana. In addition, they are less likely than their parents even today to approve of sex before marriage and having children out of wedlock. Teens want to reduce the amount of violence on TV, seek clear rules to live by, and promote the teaching of values in school. They are searching eagerly for religious and spiritual moorings in their lives. They want abstinence taught in school, and they think divorces should be harder to get."

Researchers would not have said this about Boomers forty years ago. Twenty years ago, in the Gen-X youth era, they wouldn't have even bothered to ask about it.

Millennials and Pressure

Stress has become the daily reality of Millennials' lives. Their new digital technologies place more demands on them. Their schools place more demands on them. Most importantly, their own ambitions (and their parents' ambitions for them) place more demands on them. Millennials' awareness that their peers are just as ambitious and hard working as they are—and are competitors for grades, college admissions, jobs, and careers—ramps up the stress to a higher pitch.

They know the stakes are high, and they perceive that the price of any mistake—whether getting a less-than-stellar grade or getting your name taken at an underage keg party—is more consequential than it used to be. A growing number of teens believe that what a high school junior does this week determines where he or she will be five and ten years from now. The belief that near-term achievement determines long-term success is a new teen perception—one not widely shared forty years ago.

In the 1960s and '70s, Boomers felt *decreasing* pressure to achieve. Back when JFK-era hopes of a gleaming technocracy ran aground on Vietnam, youth riots, credibility gaps, and energy crises, Boomers perceived their future growing more chaotic, less linked to work or credentials, and less subject to institutional rules. A common youth view was that you could do almost anything you wanted in high school or (especially) college and not expect that your life would be all that affected by it.

Gen Xers inherited those trends and stepped into this mindset. While they were in school, the defining symptom of teen alienation was the widespread perception that success was pretty much random in a fast-moving, risk-rewarding economy that offered a lot more opportunities than guarantees to young people. With this mindset, long preparation often seemed like a waste of time; what mattered was street smarts and a bit of luck.

For Millennials, the connection between today's behavior and tomorrow's payoff is returning. In the Datatel 2006 College Parent Survey, parents overwhelmingly agreed that today's students push themselves harder and organize themselves more than the parents themselves did at the same age—and also that they push their kids harder and pressure them more to organize than their own parents ever did with them.

Rather than breed a sense of entitlement, the buoyant economy has placed Millennial students into a pressure cooker. The growing flood of well-credentialed high school seniors increases competition for the best college slots. Technology, with its incessant stream of phone calls, emails and instant messages, puts still more burdens on a teenager's time. To help students cope, some schools are passing out day planners or offering classes in time management, and some parents are giving their teenagers personal management tools like

Sean Covey's best-selling *The 7 Habits of Highly Effective Teens: The Ultimate Teenage Success Guide*. To help themselves cope, students are multi-tasking like never before. An MTV survey of how much time teenagers spend on various activities added up to twenty-six hours each day—not including sleep.

David Brooks coined the term "organization kids" to describe the new on-campus mindset, whose common formula is: Success in life is the reward for effort plus planning. Many of today's collegians feel stressed in ways that their college-educated parents never felt during their time on campus. The classic Gen-X doctrine—that a person can always rebound from failure—seems far less plausible. As Millennials apply to college with essays about personal hard-ships, their credentials and reputation (in testimonials from school counselors) matter more than ever before. Grade grubbing has become standard practice, resume-building a stressful arms race, SAT Saturday a moment of high anxiety.

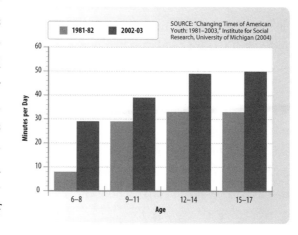

SOURCE: "Changing Times of American Youth: 1981–2003," Institute for Social Research, University of Michigan (2004)

◀ **Figure 19**

Average Daily Minutes of Homework on Weekdays, 1981–82 and 2002–03

If many college-graduating Millennials are coming home to live with their parents (unlike Gen Xers, they can't fairly be called "Boomerang kids," since many never really left home to begin with), it's not because they want to mooch, but rather because they want to avoid making a wrong career choice at a fateful point in their lives.

When Boomers graduated from college in the 1960s and '70s, young people commonly looked upon their first job or two as no big deal, not necessarily part of some pre-defined ladder to success. Young Boomers often charted their future course by their own internal compasses, asking how a path felt more than what all the signposts said. That was part of the generational rebellion against what they perceived to be the "duty-bound" lives of their parents. Since then, many Boomers have been driven to choose specialties and careers that in some way have felt like personal vocations, even "callings."

The Millennial world is quite different. They prefer timetables and milestones to mere inspiration. Today's recent graduates are likely to look upon the first job or two as extremely important, the crucial first steps in a rigorously planned path to success. Taking a job outside your field—or, worse, the "wrong first job" in your field—is to be avoided at all costs. A common long-term goal is to strike a reasonable balance between what the real world requires and what it allows.

The majority of today's high school students say they have detailed five- and ten-year plans for their future. Most have given serious thought to college financing, degrees, salaries, and employment trends. Often, they start thinking about colleges and employers before the end of the ninth grade—and collegians start thinking about grad school and careers during their first college years. In the Chartwells 2006 College Student Survey, today's undergrads agree by a six-to-one margin that they spend more time planning for the future than their parents did at the same age. Millennials see these preparations as serious and important, but not exactly fun. The share of students who "try to do my best in school" keeps going up, but so does—among boys especially—the share who don't like school either "very much" or "at all."

From the earliest grades forward, constant pressure keeps Millennials moving, busy, and purposeful. Each year, the pressure builds. In 2000, a New York Times story described how a new high-stakes test for fourth graders—failed by many—was giving elementary school children an early dose of performance anxiety. As one parent put it, "what used to happen to us at the college level has now been brought down to fifth grade. The whole feeling is much more pressure, pressure, pressure."

Grade inflation is continuing its three-decade-long trend. By 1998, one-third of all eighth graders, and one-fourth of all tenth graders, reported receiving an "A" or "A-" average. Those high grades have followed them through secondary school. From 1996 to 2006, the percentage of SAT test-takers who reported grade averages of A- through A+ grew from 36 percent to 43 percent. The impact of all those A's is simply to magnify the penalty of the occasional

Chartwells 2006
College Student Survey

The Chartwells 2006 College Student Survey, released by LifeCourse Associates and Crux research, explores the new generational traits of Millennial collegians—what differentiates them from older generations at the same age, what they want in a college, and how they feel about the cost of college and student debt. The study results highlight the upcoming changes that higher education will face as Millennials with Gen-X rather than Boomer parents fill America's campuses in the years ahead. The following are a sampling of the results of these surveys.

Millennials at College

Millennials agree that they face greater pressures than prior generations of collegians.

- Eighty-five percent say that having a college degree is more important today than it was for their parents' generation.
- They agree (69 to 6 percent) that the college application process is more stressful today than it was for their parents' generation.
- They agree (58 to 8 percent) that college is more academically challenging today than it was for their parents' generation.
- They agree (64 to 11 percent) that today's young people spend more time planning for the future than their parents' generation did at the same age.

Today's students are thinking financially during the college application process. When evaluating colleges:

- They agree (62 to 8 percent) that the earnings capability of graduates is very or extremely important.
- They agree (82 to 7 percent) that the final cost of attendance is very or extremely important.
- They agree (70 to 11 percent) that the amount of debt they are likely to have is very or extremely important.

These financial priorities reflect Millennials' overall concern about the rising cost of college. Forty percent say that paying for college will be a very or extremely difficult financial burden for them, and over half say that their debt burden will affect their career choices. On average, students expect to acquire debts of nearly $20,000.

Nonetheless, this generation of students remains career-oriented and confident about their futures. Nearly nine out of ten feel at least somewhat confident that their future earnings will be enough to justify the cost of college. Nearly five out of six say they are attending college to prepare for a specific career and to earn a higher salary. They overwhelmingly agree (97 percent) that colleges should play a significant role in helping students find jobs.

To the extent that students are aware of a long-term trend, an overwhelming majority believe that today's parents are more involved in helping their children succeed than the parents of their parents' generation. The close relationship between Millennials and their mothers and fathers is changing what these students expect from their relationships with college professors. When evaluating a college, 57 percent consider the amount of time full-time faculty spend with students very or extremely important, while only 10 percent consider it not very important.

The Gen-X factor

Children of Gen Xers expressed an even stronger sense than children of Boomers that their parents were highly involved in their lives and likely to intervene frequently. These students were more likely to say that their parents helped them choose their academic majors and individual courses. They had higher expectations that parents would intervene when they encounter problems at school, from unfair grades to class attendance issues, and (especially) with housing problems.

Millennials with Gen-X parents feel a greater desire to achieve, and more intense pressure in the college application process. They were nearly twice as likely as students with Boomer parents to apply to five or more colleges. They were also much more likely to go to school less than one hour drive away from home, implying greater family closeness.

Practical issues of post-graduate employment and student debt weighed more heavily on students with Gen-X parents than on students with Boomer parents. They were nearly twice as likely to say that student debts will affect their career choices. They were more likely to evaluate colleges based on the earnings capabilities of graduates and the percentage of graduates who pursue careers in their fields of study.

The Gender Divide

The priorities of male collegians were more social than those of their female counterparts. More males said they attended college to meet new people, have fun socially, and become well-rounded people. Nearly three times as many males rated finding a potential spouse or life-partner as a very important reason for attending college. Considerably more males than females considered the alumni network as an important inducement for enrolling—something colleges can consider as they develop strategies to attract and retain more male students.

Male students showed the most enduring reliance on parents. Men were more likely than women to expect parental assistance and involvement after graduation, and more likely to say they would live at home with their parents after completing their education. Many more males expected help from their parents with finding a job and with personal finance.

Women showed a greater connection with parents through person-to-person communication. Female collegians were more likely than males to talk with parents on the phone, receive in-person visits from them, and return home to visit. Females were more likely to go to college less than an hour drive from their parents' home, while males were more than twice as likely to go to college ten or more hours away.

Summary

Millennial collegians are pressured, career-oriented, concerned about the rising costs of college, and close with their protective parents. These trends are even more pronounced in students with Gen-X parents, who will become the majority on campuses over the next few years.

B or C. This reinforces the Millennials' fear of failure, their aversion to risk (including boundary-pushing creativity), and their desire to fit into the mainstream. Long-time teachers report that today's students are better prepared and organized than Generation X, and often know more, but that they are also less willing to take risks, be creative, and think "outside the box."

Millennials do well under pressure—but pressure (like sheltering) can sometimes be excessive, leading to negative consequences for their health. While time pressure prevents the majority of Millennials from getting enough exercise, the pressure to win athletic scholarships and prizes pushes a significant minority to overspecialize in a single sport, leading to the rise of repetitive stress injuries. Emotional distress that leads to life-threatening behaviors (suicide, violent crime, heavy substance abuse) is declining. But the frequency of eating disorders, sleep deprivation, and cutting is rising—as a rising share of teens try to cope with stress through obsessive rituals of self-control.

To many Millennial teens, it's as though a giant generational train is leaving the station. Either they're on the platform, on time and with their ticket punched, or they'll miss the train and never be able to catch up.

Millennials and Achievement

Thirty years ago, many a Boomer had big plans. So does many a Millennial today—but that's where the similarity ends.

As Boomers moved through school—from the first "free speech" movement in 1964 to the widespread adoption of pass-fail systems in the late 1970s—students expressed a growing resistance to being graded or ranked or categorized by the "system" for their achievements. Boomers preferred to be judged by who they were on the inside.

As Millennials have moved through school, they have been pushing in the opposite direction. Students are worrying more about their grades, training harder for aptitude tests, and often even begging teachers to "evaluate" them before the score is due. Adults are accommodating this trend by handing out a widening torrent of grades, stars, trophies, buttons, ribbons, and weekly on-line interim reports—so that even one-week summer camps feature endless rankings and prizes. Millennials prefer to be judged by what they do on the outside.

In college, young Boomers made their biggest mark in the arts and humanities. As young professionals, many of them became precocious leaders in the media, teaching, advertising, religion—anything having to do with the creative rearrangement of values and symbols. Millennial teens show the opposite bent. Surveys reveal that they like math and science courses best, and the traditional humanities least. They like to spend free time in shared activities with friends, instead of doing imaginative tasks on their own.

When Boomers were in school, most achievement test scores showed a decline at every age as each passing Boomer cohort reached that age. When Millennials have been in school, by contrast, most of the news on achievement test scores has been positive. The average SAT score fell almost every year from the mid-1960s to 1979, just when Boomers were reaching their late teens. Since the early 1990s, the SAT scores have risen dramatically, thanks to late-wave Gen Xers (and Millennials). In 2006, when the average SAT score unexpectedly fell from 2005 (probably due to the new test format, since the average ACT score continued to rise that year), it still exceeded the score for every earlier year since 1974. In the math l component today's scores are the highest in the history of the SAT. Scores are rising even as a much larger share of high school juniors and seniors (just over 45

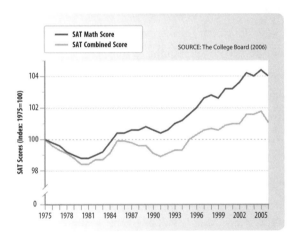

◀ **Figure 20**

Average SAT Scores of Entering College Classes Since 1975 (Index, 1975=100)

percent) are taking the exam than took it back in the early '70s (roughly 30 percent)—including millions of poor and nonwhite youths, and the offspring of recent immigrants, who, back in the '60s and '70s, never would have tested at all.

Compared with earlier generations, Millennials have shown greater improvement in math than in verbal achievement. They have also shown greater improvement in younger than in older grades, indicating a rising achievement trend by birth cohort. According to the National Assessment of Educational Progress (NAEP), which tests students nationally at age 9, age 13, and age 17, math scores have improved from the 1970s and 1980s for all three ages. For age 9 and age 13 they are the highest they have ever been. Reading scores have risen for age 9 and held steady at older ages. The NAEP also shows a narrowing achievement gap between racial and ethnic groups—meaning that black and Latino kids have been improving their scores more than white kids.

The Trends in International Math and Science Study (TIMSS) also reports steady or rising achievement since 1995 in math and science. Eighth graders have moved from below to above the international average, and for first time in 2003, American students outscored Russians (whose world-class reputation for math and science prowess once intimidated young Boomers).

The fact that verbal scores have remained constant may in part reflect the fact that, for this generation, reading and writing have assumed new aspects that are not being included in the tests. From web browsing to word processing to desktop publishing, today's students are adding new layers to the verbal skill sets that were taught to Boomers and Gen Xers at the same age. To date, the national assessments have had difficulty measuring these new skills—in particular, the SAT writing exam, which requires students to write a twenty-five-minute essay in longhand, a task few of them ever have to do in class (or will have to do in the workplace).

Regardless of one's interpretation of test results, a solid consensus exists among K-12 educators that there is much room for improvement. High school dropout rates, while recently falling, remain distressingly high (especially for minorities). Among students who graduate from high school with good grades, a large share remain academically underprepared. Employers regularly complain that a high school degree does not qualify a young worker to advance beyond an entry-level job, and well over half of all college instructors say they spend at least part of their time teaching material that should have been taught by twelfth grade. Yet most of the public alarm over these shortcomings is driven by rising expectations about what the educational system should deliver to Millennials, not by objective evidence that it worked any better for earlier generations of youth.

Whatever the K-12 system's shortcomings, no one can blame them on Millennials, whose desire to achieve and succeed within the system exceeds that of any other youth generation in living memory. This desire is reflected in the unprecedented and still-rising share of high school students who aspire to go to four-year colleges, who take Advanced Placement courses and exams, and who sign up for academic summer camps and non-remedial summer school. Cynicism about school is passé. According to the 2005–06 Horatio Alger survey, 79 percent of high school students feel motivated or inspired to work hard. According to the 2005 High School Survey of Student Engagement, two-thirds say they take pride in their school work and place a high value on learning.

Many Millennials (urban minority teens, especially) feel that a major problem with the system is that it doesn't ask enough from them. The Horatio Alger survey found that 79 percent of high school students "feel strongly" that they would respond to higher academic standards by working harder. According to the National Governors Association, two-thirds say they would work harder if high school offered more demanding and interesting courses. A decisive majority supports standardized testing. Public Agenda has found that 80 percent would support higher academic standards even if it meant required summer school for those who fell short.

On the whole, Millennial dropouts reveal a similar attitude. In a recent survey of high school dropouts age 16 to 25, two-thirds say they would have would have worked harder if more had been demanded of them academically. Nearly all express remorse for not completing their degree, and most say it was a mistake for the schools to let them to "slip by." The remarkable success of "early college"—a rapidly expanding program in many states that takes high school student at risk of dropping out and enrolls them in college courses—shows how positively Millennials respond to high standards and to high expectations.

Millennials keep striving for achievement even when engaged in entirely optional activities outside the formal school curriculum. In high schools and colleges, the quality and professionalism of extracurricular (what some call "co-curricular") programs is rising rapidly—from student governments to yearbooks and newspapers, self-produced radio and TV shows, theater productions, videogame tournaments, specialized sports programs, and profitable student-run businesses. Unprecedented numbers of students are bringing their organizing and high-tech skills to community service, sometimes even replacing adult professionals. Those who enter competitions for spelling, geography, science, music, history, debating, or anything else—and who want to have any realistic chance of winning—must excel at a level unimaginable in prior decades. For earlier generations, much of what young people did outside of school was said to be "unstructured" and "informal." We no longer use such words to describe the intensity and specialization with which Millennials approach most of the activities in their lives.

DeWitt Clinton, an inner-city high school in the Bronx, looks like many other such schools in the Millennial era—crowded, ringed with metal detectors, teeming with busy teens. DeWitt Clinton also enables over half of its incoming freshmen to go on to college and has been repeatedly voted one of the most improved schools in the nation. Homework is due in every class every day. Grades are based only on results, not aptitude or effort. The buildings bustle with high-octane extracurriculars. The school's mission statement begins: "We believe that high expectations plus high standards equals high achievement." By this standard, Millennials are achieving more—both in school and out—than other recent generations of youth.

Millennials are already the largest, most studious, and best-prepared pool of college applicants ever—and in the years ahead those trends will only broaden and deepen. Not only is their generation as huge as Boomers were in youth, but an astounding 70 percent of its high school graduates plan to continue their education in some form after high school.

Where their Boomer parents initiated an array of negative behavioral trends as youths—in crime, suicide, accidents, substance abuse, and sexual risk-taking—Millennials are pushing all those same trends in a positive direction.

Yet with this good news come new challenges. Millennials and their parents can be very demanding—a trend that is likely to escalate over the next several years, as Gen Xers increasingly replace Boomers among the ranks of collegiate parents. Millennials and their parents tend to be fixated on having only the "best" of this or that. They place enormous emphasis of the quality of campus life—from the strength of school spirit to the safety of dorms to the quality of mental health services and mentoring programs. They consult the doctor-lawyer-counselor "team" if things don't go well.

Part Two

While the rising demand for a college education may allow some institutions of higher learning to become choosier about which applicants they admit, the applicants and their parents are becoming choosier about what they demand from higher education. Their list of perceived "needs" could bankrupt even the wealthiest of universities. Among their more real needs is to find affordable tuition (perhaps with a discount, alias a "scholarship") and to avoid crushing student loans—or, at the other end, to avoid feeling like the only person in the dorm who is paying "full freight."

Meanwhile, many institutions confront a very real cost squeeze. While some private colleges are hugely endowed, most are not—and are under pressure to match their wealthier rivals in facilities and services. Many public institutions are facing new budget cuts or tuition hikes mandated by legislatures in a time of flat or declining tax revenues. As Gen Xers rise in political power, from state legislatures to the U.S. Congress, the political scrutiny and demand for institutional accountability will increase. Meanwhile, new market competitors, also driven by Gen Xers, may start offering lower-cost alternatives to the traditional higher education models of the past century.

Taken together—and combined with the parental closeness and media glare that accompanies these young people wherever they go—this adds up to a very difficult set of choices for every institution from the smallest of colleges to the largest of universities. Unless the economy grows beyond what anyone can reasonably plan, none will simply be able to "ride it out." Tough choices will have to be made.

What should a college do to cope with these new students—and to prepare for the onslaught of the even more Millennial-style classes to come? How should admissions, campus life, and the classroom experience be altered? Where should new money be spent? In this era of parent-child co-purchasing, these are questions with two sets of answers—one set involving the students themselves, and the other involving their parents.

In the next set of chapters, we address the student side. Here, the seven core Millennial traits hold the key. For each, we explore the impact of this new generation on institutions of higher education—and the implications for recruiting and admissions, campus life, and the classroom.

Some of these choices will be obvious, and others controversial. Many administrators and faculty members, might prefer to resist a number of Millennial trends. That happens with every new generation. To some degree, this resistance can be constructive, even necessary—after all, it is the role of universities to mentor young people according to timeless standards of character, and of professors to teach according to the timeless standards of their disciplines. But past a certain point, resistance from older generations can impede young people from pursuing a fresh agenda. In the end (as America learned in the 1960s), it will be the rising generation of youth—their goals, talents, and sensibilities—that will lead the way to a new future.

6 | Special

"Child-centered we indubitably are, like no other people at no other time in history…. It's in the air, the culture: Children, in America, now rule."

— JOSEPH EPSTEIN (2006)

Special

As a generation, Millennials feel a specialness that started with the devotion of parents and families and has since worked its way out into our national civic life. Since birth, older generations have instilled in them the sense that they are the personal focus of adult inspiration and are collectively vital to the nation. Through laws like *No Child Left Behind*, and principles like the Gates Foundation's commitment to make "every child" college ready, America has concentrated its attention on improving the quality of the K-12 education of each of these very special children.

Now that Millennials are passing through college, they, their parents—and the nation—expect institutions of higher learning to treat them the same way. In precept if not in law, *No Child Left Behind* is coming to college.

This has enormous implications for institutions of higher learning. In the years ahead, a college or university can no longer assume that its ability to market to new recruits will be sustained by its traditional reputation, the success of its alumni, or, put simply, the power of its brand. In the years to come, colleges will have to sell parents on the idea that an institution is precisely fitted to protect and educate their very "special" child. On the one hand, recruiting Millennials will require an array of personalized amenities to which these Millennials, and their parents, feel they are entitled. On the other hand, it will also require an explicit appeal to a fresh sense of civic purpose—a strategy that would have rolled the eyes of many in the Gen-X youth era.

Implications for Recruiting and Admissions

The mutual perception of specialness by college applicants and parents helps explain why co-purchasing is today so prevalent in the choice of college. Just as teens and parents jointly participate in the purchase of a son's clothes and a daughter's car (or a mom's computer), so too are parents and high-school seniors jointly making college decisions.

Recruiting materials and tours should overtly acknowledge this trend. College brochures should show more adults than before and highlight features that may appeal less to students than to anxious parents—features like optimized "life plans," close supervision, and full-spectrum medical and counseling services, especially for students with disabilities of various kinds.

Parental involvement cannot be allowed to go too far. Many schools are discovering cases where parents have essentially "hijacked" the application process, asking all the questions on campus tours, showing up at information sessions without their sons and daughters, filling out the forms, editing application essays, and perhaps even writing them. Colleges can combat this by encouraging students to engage more actively in their own college decisions, offering separate campus tours for students and parents, and communicating with students by email rather than by hard-copy letters that are often opened and seen first by parents, and being very explicit about the limits of parental help with essays.

The best permanent solution to the interfering-parent problem is to establish a formal division of labor between the college and the parents, in which colleges welcome parental participation in certain areas, but not in others.

Many administrators complain about the "softness" of today's students, and their sense of entitlement to an astonishing array of creature comforts. There is some truth to this. While growing up, this generation has already gotten plenty of special treatment from parents who think it's OK for their kids to be given a little more, given how much more is being expected of them. The attitude does not change once Millennials reach college. Today's youth-focused America delights in learning about the special amenities Millennials enjoy—for example, reading through the four full-color pages *Newsweek* recently dedicated to the furnishings that college-bound characters from the television show "The O.C." would bring to their dorms in the next season.

These expectations are spurring a new battle of luxury perks in college admissions, in which colleges compete to offer ever more lavish items to Millennials students. One large state university recently added free computers, printers, and micro-fridges to its dorm rooms, along with delivered, personalized birthday cakes. "This is what students expect," commented a university spokesperson. The high-end "arms race" will allow colleges without strong brand recognition to distinguish themselves from their competitors. Looking ahead, colleges should keep a close eye on how much these luxuries cost and what value they are really offering. As Gen Xers fill the ranks of college parents, ROI (return on tuition investment) will be in the forefront of their minds—and, hence, should be at the forefront of each college's recruiting agenda.

In the years to come, colleges will discover yet another way into Millennials' hearts—through their stomachs. Students perusing such tools as the *Princeton Review's* guide to the "Best 361 Colleges" can now scroll down a list of the twenty schools rated highest for dining. Today's pre-college youths spend less time eating than those of prior decades. Even more than older Americans, today's collegians have largely lost the custom of formal sit-down meals and want food, including complete meals, to be available as close to 24/7 (and as convenient to dorms) as possible. Yet as they spend less time eating, they eat more. Features like lavish dessert buffets, bread bars, all-you-can-eat pasta stations, and diverse ethnic cuisines have become standard. To add the special personal touch, a growing number of colleges invite students' parents send in recipes ("Jason's mom's lasagna")—which often turn out to be big hits. Colleges have to strike the difficult balance between feeding Millennials what, when, and where they want, while at the same time helping them battle the fitness and obesity challenges facing many in this generation.

Millennials also want to go to a college where they will be prepared to play a special role in the world. Stressing an institution's traditions, high standards, and involvement in national life is important for appealing both to Millennials themselves and to their parents. With young adults thinking long-term and Boomer parents talking "legacy," recruiting messages should become less personal and more historical. Recruiting materials should dare to be earnest in highlighting school history, institutional heritage, student organizations, and ties to the local community. Millennials can be most effectively portrayed in collective images. Photos of energized teams engaging in a campus-wide activity will work better than images of a lone scholar lost in thought, studying in the library or on the campus green.

More than other generations, Millennials will be attracted by personalized attention and recognition in the recruitment process. Some colleges send students "v.i.p." applications with the student's personal information already filled out, along with a personalized email congratulating her or him for having been specially selected—an effective tactic for a generation used to personal attention. Some colleges try to make a personal connection with prospective students years before they apply—a strategy that CEO Brian Niles of TargetX calls the new "Recruiting 2.0 Revolution."

The Millennial sense of entitlement can bring a reaction from rejected students (and parents) who are not accustomed to failure. College admissions officers report an increase in the number of parents calling to complain to colleges that reject their child. With the arrival of Gen-X parents, complaining phone calls could increasingly be replaced by legal challenges—which are now said to be far more common than before in K-12 schools. To protect themselves, colleges need to set clear admission rules, follow those rules, and develop ways to document that their committees are following those rules.

Implications for Campus Life

On freshman arrival day, college presidents give moms and dads the usual warm speeches about "up to now it's been your turn, now it's our turn." Today a new twist is required. Not only are colleges having to pay more attention to parents when recruiting, they are also finding ways to enable parental engagement after the child is enrolled. Many of today's parents have so much invested, emotionally and financially, in their children's well-being that they cannot quickly relinquish their roles. This requires colleges and universities to negotiate carefully with parents, manage their expectations, and understand that

Guides to Helicopter Parenting

Sample titles since the first Millennials arrived on campus:

Title	Author(s)
When Your Kid Goes to College: A Parent's Survival Guide	Carol Barkin
You're On Your Own (But I'm Here if You Need Me): Mentoring Your Child During the College Years	Marjorie Savage
Don't Tell Me What to Do, Just Send Money: The Essential Parenting Guide to the College Years	Helen E. Johnson
Been There, Should've Done That II: More Tips for Making the Most of College	Suzette Tyler
Almost Grown: Launching Your Child from High School to College	Patricia Pasick
Empty Nest…Full Heart: The Journey from Home to College	Andrea Van Steenhouse
When You're Facing the Empty Nest: Avoiding Midlife Meltdown When Your Child Leaves Home	Mary Ann Froehlich
She's Leaving Home: Letting Go As Daughter Goes To College	Connie Jones
The Launching Years: Strategies for Parenting from Senior Year to College Life	Laura Kastner
I'll Miss You Too: An Off-to-College Guide for Parents and Students	Margo E. Woodacre Bane
For Parents Only: Tips for Surviving the Journey from Homeroom to Dorm Room	Julia Johnson and Mary Kay Shanley

many of them may be trying to share as much as possible in their sons' and daughters' rite of passage.

As helicopter parents—always hovering, ultra-protective, unwilling to let go—Boomers are constantly asserting their children's special needs and interests. The impact of helicopter parents will be particularly strong when dealing with "special needs" students, more of whom are diagnosed every year. As Gen-X "stealth-fighter" parents enter the college scene over the coming years, colleges should expect these trends to intensify.

Just as one would expect from a generation that has always celebrated itself, Boomer parents often regard college as more about themselves than about their kids. The challenge for a college is to enable Boomer parents to refresh their personal connection with college life without interfering with the day-to-day experience of their collegiate children. There are many good ways of doing this.

Programs for parents (with titles like "Parents' College Transition") have multiplied since the first Millennials arrived at college, from a dozen or so in 1999 to over three hundred today. Washington University in St. Louis now has an email newsletter for parents, "Family Ties," and Colorado College will offer brief courses for parents who want a taste of their children's educational experience. West Virginia University has created a new salaried position, the Parent Advocate, who fields roughly four thousand calls a year on the school's Parent Club Helpline. In 2002, *College Parent Magazine* launched its first edition under the slogan "everything you need to survive the college parenting experience."

When confronting hyper-involved parents, college should not block their efforts (which only fuels resentment), nor give them comprehensive sway. Instead, the solution is to channel parental energy, encouraging parents to involve themselves in certain areas of college life while giving the college jurisdiction over others. This will allow the school to satisfy the demands of parents while still fulfilling its role as an institution. Some colleges ask all parents and students to sign a "relationship covenant" to establish what is expected of each party.

Figure 21 ▶

Percent of Incoming Freshman Class with Parent Having at Least a College Degree, 1972–2005

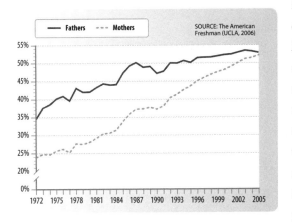

Schools can also give parents special readings or videos about how they can help their child in the right way. Some colleges (like summer camps) email parents occasional videos of campus life. A few are installing permanent web cams on the campus green so that parents can "tune in" whenever they want—and so that their children can set up "appointments" to stop by the camera and wave.

On their own, Millennials will be enough to handle.

They have very high expectations for housing. Millennials are less comfortable with roommates than their parents were—in part because they are unfamiliar with them. One college survey found that three-quarters of incoming freshmen have never shared a room with anyone, not even a sibling. Though double-occupancy remains the on-campus norm for most freshmen (in private colleges it is often required), students after their first year generally prefer single occupancy. Yet even upperclassmen want plenty of group space close to their rooms for socializing or studying. The most popular dorms feature four to ten students in small solo bedrooms (or partitionable double bedrooms) clustered apartment-style, where each cluster or "pod" or "super suite" shares several bathrooms, a kitchen large enough for group cooking, and a spacious common area with plenty of light, comfortable furniture, and a theater/media center comparable to what most of them grew up with at home. Colleges have noted a new resistance to group bathrooms in a generation that is not accustomed to having anyone else present when showering or even using sinks.

To meet Millennial expectations, the quality of old-style residence halls will have to improve. Every residence hall built since 2002 has been equipped with air conditioning and high-speed Internet access. Suites and clustered apartments are overwhelmingly replacing the old cramped doubles along one hall with poor ventilation and limited wiring. Meanwhile, Millennial collegians are filling their improved living spaces with a stunning array of personal amenities. Between 2003 and 2005, spending on school-related items rose by 33 percent, with particular increases in high-priced items like cell phones, laptops, and portable vacuums. Millennial students are abandoning the extra-long, extra-narrow beds that parents may remember. "They're looking for amenities, and double beds are one of them," said Don Kamalsky, director of student housing at Case Western University.

When students can't get the kinds of accommodations and amenities they want on campus, many turn to off-campus housing—especially to the large new "edge campus" apartment complexes springing up around major state universities. Some parents are purchasing properties close to campus where their children can live comfortably all four years, after which the parents expect to sell the property at a profit. Public colleges, half of which house no more than

30 percent of their students on campus (at private colleges the figure is 70 percent), are now actively competing with off-campus private developers in price and quality to win back students and bolster their on-campus student presence.

Where colleges succeed in retaining or winning back Millennials, chief housing officers typically stress (both to parents and to their parents) the benefits of belonging to a strong college community, the positive impact of on-campus living on academic performance, and concerns over safety and security. While today's students demand quality housing and amenities, they also want to feel connected with their peers, to excel in the classroom, and to lessen their risk of violence or injury. *USA Today* recently reported that the number of fire-related student fatalities off-campus—nearly all of them during late-night hours—dwarfs the number in on-campus housing.

To satisfy both demands—great amenities and a protected community—some colleges are allowing private developers to build apartment-style housing on university property and lease it out to students. This enables students to live with other students in the center of college life, while paying rent to a private landlord and living in housing much more luxurious than the traditional '70's-style cinder-block halls—and without requiring the college to raise housing fees for all students.

Implications for the Classroom

Many of these issues of heavy parental involvement are also affecting academic life. Moms and dads are showing up at course registrations and advisor meetings with their kids, and sometimes even without them. The cell phone, which one academic dean calls "the world's longest umbilical cord," is a constant presence. As parents' involvement escalates, colleges can construct gentle barriers against moms and dads who might otherwise interfere with learning. The University of Vermont has introduced "parent bouncers," students trained to divert parents who attend course registration and explain diplomatically that they are not invited to help choose courses.

The Millennials' close personal ties to their parents influence what they expect from their professors. Kids who grew up with "attachment parenting" often look for "attachment teaching." In the Chartwells 2006 College Student Survey, 57 percent considered the amount of time they spend with full-time faculty to be "very" or "extremely" important. More then Gen Xers, Millennials want to visit professors outside class hours and consult with them about personal challenges and life plans. To satisfy this desire, colleges can offer smaller class sizes, freshman seminars, more faculty office hours, and specific requirements for faculty members to advise (or mentor) individual students outside the classroom.

Throughout their K-12 education, teachers have discovered that Millennials perform best when given constant feedback on their academic performance. Middle and high schools that have earned award-winning reputations for improving learning outcomes typically use continuous weekly monitoring of every student's progress in the classroom as a cornerstone of their teaching method. This includes tight cycles of feedback or redirection. Computerized or on-line lesson plans follow a similar strategy. When Millennials enter college, they continue to associate cutting-edge education with an emphasis on structure and feedback. For this generation, evaluation is not just about getting a grade at the end of a course. It is an essential part of the learning process. Professors who rely on end-of-semester sink-or-swim exams or on creative projects designed to "spread the class out" could trigger anxiety, and even active resistance, from Millennials and their parents.

Partly because of the high tuition they pay and their taste for digital multimedia, but mostly because of their collective sense of specialness, Millennials widely assume that they deserve the best possible classroom instruction. They think high-quality tech-aided student learning should be at the very top of their college's agenda. They will not hesitate to express their high expectations for classes and professors—and their disapproval when those expectations aren't met. The past few years have seen a proliferation of web sites (like *rate myprofessors.com* or the edgier *myprofessorsucks.com*) that allow students to publicly rate professors on everything from material to preparation to speaking style. Some sites are local to college communities, while others are international. To marginalize these sites, colleges can set and enforce their own standards for quality classroom teaching, which can reassure students and their parents that student feedback is taken seriously and that the college never puts reputation and research ahead of the undergraduate learning experience.

7 | Sheltered

"We have been hearing much of late about a return to the in loco parentis approach that fell out of favor in the late 1960s. The same Baby Boomers who fought to end these restrictions want to bring them back, perhaps out of dismay that their own children may have to make some of the same mistakes that they did."

— JUDITH SHAPIRO, PRESIDENT OF BARNARD COLLEGE (2002)

Sheltered

Millennials have grown up watching perimeters rise around all aspects of their lives. Everywhere they go—from childhood to adolescence to young adulthood—they expect to be kept safe. College is no exception. Already, dormitories have tighter-than-ever security (in the Boomer college days, they often had none), with most campuses converting to hotel-style keycards and ubiquitous surveillance cams. On the one hand, parents want their collegiate children to inhabit ivy-wrapped gothic buildings; on the other, they worry about the healthfulness of what's inside, from water to ventilation. Today's collegians comply easily with restrictions that Boomers or Gen Xers at that age would have assailed as arbitrary, intrusive, or violative of their rights. Indeed, Millennials trust parents and other authority figures far more than those parents and authorities did themselves when they themselves were young. Today's undergraduates have grown accustomed to this emphasis on protection. This helps explains why they are more risk averse, more careful, more confined, and more sedentary than young people used to be.

Implications for Recruiting and Admissions

Campus security is now a sales point, and the lack of it can be a real hindrance. To some degree, each college is a prisoner of its own geography, but no matter where a college may be located, it can implement the state-of-the-art, high-tech security many students and parents now expect. Accountability is key, and today's applicants (and parents) can assess the facts for any college, including recent crime trends, at the federal Campus Security Statistics Web site. Colleges with a solid record of student safety can tout this advantage explicitly in their recruiting. One small college in Iowa that had long fielded a small plain-clothed security force put its officers in uniform to make security more conspicuously present to collegians and visiting parents.

Families are factoring safety issues like campus alcohol abuse into the college selection process. The group "Mothers Against Drunk Driving" now ranks colleges based on how effectively they limit student drinking. In the Boomer or Gen-X era, schools that cracked down on alcohol might have deterred applicants—now they can use it as a strategy to attract students.

With Millennials on campus, any lapse of safety, security, or student discipline will bring far more media attention than in earlier decades. The 2006 allegations against the Duke lacrosse team provoked an enormous media response, whereas the 1999 bonfire collapse that killed twelve Texas A&M students was a far smaller story. Because of society's special concern for Millennials, media scrutiny about safety will continue to escalate in the coming years, and any broadly reported stories about campus crimes, suicides, accidents, or other tragedies will be more likely to damage an institution's reputation among applicants.

The search for a sheltered environment may increase the appeal of community colleges and small colleges relatively close to home. Many schools have long debated whether to be a "college" or a "university." Through the Boomer and Gen-X collegiate eras, the tide moved in favor of "university" and all that this word implies—a big, cosmopolitan, anonymous, professionalized place bustling with prestigious research. With Millennials, that tide may be shifting. The very words "community" and "college" may lose their provincial stigma by projecting many of the virtues Boomer parents and their collegiate sons and daughters are seeking: a feeling of close community, small class size, teachers who care and know your name, *in loco parentis* rules, core curricula, and traditions. Millennials are already experiencing this before college. Many of the most successful high schools are dividing their students into small groups (especially in the ninth grade) to provide closer surveillance and "small school" support.

To be sure, the word "university" still carries a big brand clout, implying a larger, more public institution. Many schools are understandably reluctant to abandon this label, which carries weight with Millennials. Yet even these schools may want to reorganize their internal campus into smaller entities with communal or family labels ("colleges" or "academies"), much like the tight-knit "houses" at Hogwarts School of Witchcraft and Wizardry in the Harry Potter stories so beloved by today's incoming freshmen.

The Millennials' close relationships with parents, combined with anxieties over campus security, highway safety, and global terrorism, have enhanced many colleges' ability to recruit in their own backyards. After the 9/11 attacks, students became significantly more reluctant to travel far from home. Now, five years later, the proportion of freshmen who enter colleges within fifty miles of their parents' home remains considerably higher than it was before. The shift towards local colleges has been all the more notable, considering how much cheaper and easier long-distance communication and air transportation have become in recent years.

This trend is important for study-abroad programs as well. At any time, depending on the course of events, the world could quickly become a more dangerous place for Millennial collegians than it was for young Boomers or Gen Xers. Though colleges with programs abroad are enhancing their security features, dramatic global events may overwhelm their efforts. To guard against this, a college might want to relocate overseas programs in high-risk areas—or, at least, have alternatives readily available at short notice—to reassure recruits and their parents about personal safety.

Implications for Campus Life

Far more than prior generations, Millennials are willing to relinquish some personal liberties for more security, safety, and civic order. For such a genera-tion, no campus can be too safe. In the wake of the 9/11 attacks, 47 percent of colleges and universities have significantly tightened security measures. MIT increased its security budget by $1.5 million, money that included funding for an armed guard at the university's reactor. These measures have remained in place nearly everywhere, in part because they appeal to the ongoing Millennial interest in secure campus perimeters.

Safety concerns extend to misbehavior by students themselves. Many colleges are shifting toward no-nonsense college enforcement policies, freely sharing information with local law enforcement and cracking down on rowdy students at or after athletic games. These policies are supported by Millennial youths to an extent unimaginable back when Boomers and Gen Xers were on campus. Though the data are open to interpretation, campus-based crime among collegians does appear to be dropping, just as it has been among teens and young-adults generally.

Before college, Millennials have responded to protective measures with a good record of compliance. Alcohol consumption among high school students has been declining for two decades. The percentage of freshmen who say they drank beer frequently or occasionally during their senior year of high school has fallen to its lowest level since this question was first asked in 1966. College drinking now appears to be dropping as well—partly because Millennials are less interested in casual boozing, and partly because more colleges are offering alcohol-free spaces. Many campuses are using special stamps, bracelets, and cards to keep students into or out of certain dorms or buildings at certain hours, or to enforce alcohol age laws. Increasingly, student drinking is moving off-campus, and more campuses are offering substance-free dorms, making it easier for non-drinking students to maintain that lifestyle.

Hit by news stories about excessive drinking and hazing and by the threat of catastrophic lawsuits—and after seeing their national memberships shrink by an estimated 25 percent since 1990—fraternities and sororities are working hard to rehabilitate their image. A less rambunctious style of Greek life is emerging, with tamer rushing and more emphasis on upbeat extracurricular activities. Spearheading movements like the "dry fraternity" and the "balanced man" program, Boomer administrators are trying to shelter Millennials from the Greek drinking culture they themselves intensified in their youth. After going dry in 2000, Northwestern University's the Phi Delta Theta crafted a new motto: "Brotherhood: Our Substance of Choice." At Northwestern University, Boomer administrators objected to a fraternity showing of the 1972 movie "Animal House," depicting rowdy fraternity life in the early '60s when Boomer were themselves in college. After some mild initial skepticism, Millennials largely go along with these protective initiatives. The strongest resistance comes from Gen-X alumni, who are baffled by the willing compliance of today's Greek-lifers.

Polls reveal a mixed Millennial verdict on other forms of substance abuse. On the whole, they are tolerant of casual marijuana use, but are not attracted to drugs as a lifestyle. Someone who says they have "tried" something might be cool, but someone known to do it regularly is not. Even at colleges where students are not sure whether the actual use of alcohol and other drugs is declining, there is widespread agreement that such behavior is becoming less conspicuous and is interfering less with normal student life. Prescription drug abuse is more widespread than before, mainly because so many more students have prescriptions for medications. Much of this involves so-called "smart drugs" that students take to boost their scores on exams. New fads (like ecstasy) arise from time to time, but the overall trend appears to be away from substance abuse.

The rate of smoking among high school students began falling in 1997 and has recently dropped to the lowest level ever measured. Smoking among college students began falling when Millennials reached campus in 2001 and 2002—after having risen for Gen-X undergrads, women especially, throughout the 1990s. Today's incoming Millennial freshmen are familiar with zero-tolerance smoking rules (no smoking any time, any place) at their high schools. Among today's collegians, it is generally considered rude for a smoker to light up in the presence of a non-smoker—a norm that did not exist for Boomers or Gen Xers on campus. This creates the opportunity for a college administration to establish new non-smoking rules and zones that might be more controversial among campus employees and faculty than among undergraduates.

More students are coming to campus with weight problems, reflecting a rising trend toward obesity among youth in general over the last several decades. Students sometimes overdo it at increasingly elaborate dining-hall buffets. The fabled "freshman fifteen" is enlarging into the "freshman twenty-five." To address the obesity problem, a growing number of colleges are trying to put the whole student body on a diet. George Washington University instituted a campus-wide diet menu in 2003, and students at Northeastern University can call up a nutritional analysis of dining-hall menus on a flat-screen computer kiosk. Colleges are also encouraging students to be more active. Rice lends out pedometers, urging students to log ten thousand steps a day, and Temple awards prizes for spending time at the gym.

At the other end of the eating spectrum, many Millennials skip meals or delve into harmful food fads or worse (anorexia, bulimia, or "exercise bulimia") once they are out of range of daily parental control. Residence hall assistants can watch for these problems, inquire into students' eating and exercise habits, and refer students for counseling when necessary.

Today's students are now coming to campus with more diagnosed eating restrictions—lactose intolerance, various allergies—and are insisting on access to special vegetarian or vegan foods or familiar ethnic cuisines. All these factors combine to make food delivery a far more complex and specialized task for Millennials than for prior generations. The days of mystery meat loaf are over. Too many students, and their parents, will insist on knowing exactly what's in it.

Millennial students and their parents are making major new demands on campus counseling services, even though, by objective standards, Millennials have fewer emotional problems than prior generations. For the first time in decades, the rate of youth suicide and self-reported depression is trending down. Meanwhile, addressing the emotional problems of students has become a higher priority. College counselors sometimes confuse the frequency of student visits with the severity of student problems—when often it simply reflects the greater comfort students have in talking with and depending on adults.

Most Millennials have been raised by their parents to regard health care, both physical and mental, as a continuous process of monitoring and adjustment. Over their lifetimes, they have broadly been invited to consult with credentialed professionals and to rely on their judgment about ailments that older generations would have borne without complaint. Today's collegians generally trust institutions, believe in the efficacy of health-care science, and have a low tolerance for people (including themselves) who persistently feel bad about life. Unlike Gen Xers, who wanted to be seen as tough and self-sufficient, and often regarded a visit to a counselor as a form of punishment,

Emotional Depression

Because Millennials are pressured, more incoming freshmen than ever (27 percent) report "frequently feeling overwhelmed." Because they expect others to minister to their bad feelings, more freshmen than ever (8 percent) say they "probably will use personal counseling" while at college. Because a rising share have already taken prescription medications for emotional problems while in grade school, more are taking them in college. Thanks to such medications, many students can now enroll in college who never would have applied before. Currently, 85 percent of college counseling centers report a rise in the number of students with "severe psychological problems"—where only 56 percent reported a rise in 1988.

However, Millennials in general are not more emotionally depressed and troubled than earlier student cohorts. To the contrary, the share of incoming freshmen who report "frequently feeling depressed" reached a record low (7 percent) in 2005. Nor is it true that the youth suicide rate is rising. In fact, it is falling.

	Average (%)	
	1990–1996	2006
Share of freshmen who say they are "frequently overwhelmed"	24	29
Share of freshmen who say they will likely seek "personal counseling"	4	8
Share of freshmen who say they are "frequently depressed"	9	7
	Average (n)	
	1990–1996	2006
U.S. suicides per 100,000, aged 15–19	10.7	7.3[a]
U.S. suicides per 100,000, aged 20–24	15.4	12.1

[a] For 2003

Millennials welcome the special attention. Like the fabricated characters in the popular videogame *Sims*, they await an optimal tweak on their "personal adjustment" knobs. Colleges can staff up to handle frequent counseling visits, wellness checkups, and the rapidly rising share of students who require regular prescription medication.

Much like K-12 schools before them, colleges are expected to be institutionally responsible for protecting students as though they were public property—in effect, to adopt an *in loco communitatis* doctrine of higher education. When Millennials were in grade school, poster ads, candy machines, soda pouring rights, and net marketing software came under attack from parents and community leaders. Many school districts have responded by abandoning these amenities and foregoing the extra income. Colleges now confront a similar choice. Deluxe retailers, mailing list vendors, credit card companies, and pharmaceutical companies desperately want to ply their wares to the vast new crop of undergraduates. These commercial interests can make life easier for administrators by addressing product, service, and financial needs that might otherwise require staff resources. There is a real risk to opening the gate and letting them in, however. If anything wrong comes of it, a college could have to field endless "Is it true that you allow…" queries from outraged moms and dads, muckraking journalists, and moralizing legislators.

More than ever before, parents of Millennials insist on knowing about their child's college health problems, physical and emotional—and resent any legal and bureaucratic barriers that stand in their way. With a number of schools facing massive law suits for failing to inform parents about their children's mental health problems, many colleges are doing all they can to put safety ahead of privacy. To reassure parents, avoid bad publicity, and protect themselves legally, some colleges are alerting parents and students well in advance about FERPA privacy laws and explaining how, if both parent and child wish it, all parties can sign the necessary disclosure forms. Colleges can expedite this process by making the disclosure and non-disclosure options easily accessible on-line, and by enabling their data systems to hold two sets of records, one set that can be disclosed to parents, and the other not.

With or without information provided by the college, many of today's parents try their best to remain exhaustively filled in on their sons' and daughters' lives. Students are using cell phones and emails to connect more often with their families, and increasing numbers are going home on the weekends. This is easier now that students are choosing campuses closer to their hometowns and communicating more often, not just with parents, but with other family members and with friends from high school. Schools whose students are mostly regional may find that they are becoming "suitcase colleges" that empty out on the weekends.

Implications for the Classroom

Roll call is back. A growing number of colleges are encouraging or requiring professors to take attendance in every class in order to keep closer track of student performance. Students can be failed for neglecting to show up. Attendance can be especially stressed for freshmen, who are often overwhelmed

FERPA and Boomer Parents

The Family Educational Rights and Privacy Act (FERPA) prohibits any school that receives federal funds (meaning just about any college) from releasing any part of the "educational record" of any student aged 18 or older to any outsider without the student's express permission. The "educational record" includes just about everything—grades, attendance, rule infractions, health records, and so on. To ensure this privacy, FERPA has required colleges to set up elaborate bureaucratic safeguards, along with special procedures by which students can access, amend, or appeal anything on file.

When FERPA was signed into federal law in 1974, the Watergate-stricken G.I. Generation "Establishment" was reeling and the reputation of Boomer collegians—who had just won the elimination of the military draft and a reduction in the voting age from 21 to 18—was riding high. The law's main original purpose was to keep government agencies like draft boards from prying into students' lives. The law also prevented parents from finding out what students were doing while at college. And while this was not FERPA's main purpose, most Americans believed this was just as well. In the mid-1970s, public opinion strongly supported more independence for youth, more distance between parents and kids, and a general rolling back of any *in loco parentis* role.

More than three decades have passed, and the passage of time has gradually changed Boomer minds about this law. They are no longer FERPA's protected group, but rather the group from whom others (namely, their own children) are being protected. Today, it is not uncommon for Boomer parents of Millennial collegians to demand to see their children's private records. The role of parent is sacred to many of them, and they just aren't sure if they can trust a college to replace them in that role.

The controversy hit the news in the spring of 2000, when a super-achieving 19-year-old student set herself ablaze in her dorm room at the Massachusetts Institute of Technology. Until her suicide, her parents knew nothing of her inner anguish. Furious that the university never alerted them that a school psychiatrist had considered hospitalizing their daughter, they sued MIT in a case that has drawn national media attention. In mounting a vigorous defense, the college cited its FERPA requirements as protecting it from liability. (A decision is still pending, at this writing).

What can a college do?

Take concrete steps to inform parents and students of FERPA rights and responsibilities, right at the start of the students' college careers. Make sure parents know that students may, in writing, waive FERPA rules and allow a parent or guardian to have access to their records. Make the waiver simple, so that every family that wants it can get it. The goal should be to move the controversy away from the college and back squarely to the student and parent.

Because many students will be inclined to sign waivers, often quite willingly, college information systems must adapt to larger numbers of "open record" students. Academic counselors and health professionals must be aware that any student who walks in the door may have parents who expect to be notified immediately in case of trouble. Counselors should try to keep close relationships with parents and, perhaps, with other professionals who have dealt with students previously.

Could this tension between legal requirements and changing public mores lead to the end of FERPA? Perhaps. Rather than having to deal with different categories of "waivered" and "unwaivered" students, along with legal worries about how specific each waiver must be, colleges may press Congress to relax some FERPA regulations, much as the law has already been amended to allow parental notification in the case of drug or alcohol abuse. Under a relaxed FERPA, however, colleges would have a much clearer burden to keep in touch with parents and might have to increase staff to comply. Each student's health and academic status would have to monitored and any warning signs or deviations reported to parents—quite a contrast with the college world that most of today's Gen Xers recall.

Here again, careful parent management will be one of the most nerve-wracking challenges of the Millennial college era. With or without FERPA, it is the new challenge of today's college administrators to persuade today's parents to "let go," just a little bit more with each passing year, with confidence that their come-of-age Millennial children remain in very good hands.

by the transition to college and who may need extra structure, surveillance, and feedback.

The long college week is also making a comeback. Many colleges have started scheduling Friday morning classes in a deliberate effort to curb Thursday night partying. The University of Richmond tells faculty to give quizzes during their Friday classes as an incentive for students to attend five days a week. Though Friday and even Saturday classes were common when Boomers were in college, many departments began avoiding them in the 1980s when they discovered that many Gen-X students would simply not show up. A longer work week doesn't bother Millennials as much, because they like the balance it adds to their weekly schedules.

As is true for personal safety, colleges can expect increasing scrutiny—from parents, the media, and the government—of what goes on in the classroom. The number of complaints about "unfair" grades or denials of honors could grow in the years ahead. These complaints might sometimes be accompanied by lawsuits over "capricious" and "injurious" academic evaluations filed by disappointed students and their disgruntled parents.

The same culture war that has followed Millennials through middle and high school is following them into college. News stories use words like "relativism" or "indoctrination" to alarm readers about what students claim to be hearing in their classes. The media showcase professors with unconventional views or idiosyncratic teaching methods. Colleges now find their "values" under scrutiny from parents. According to the Datatel 2006 College Parent Survey, 39 percent of parents hold views they consider to be "more conservative" than those of college faculty. (Another 19 percent of parents hold views they consider to be "more liberal.") Professors are more at risk than before of hearing complaints from parents who differ with their "ideology" or whose collegiate children report to their parents that they are getting more opinion than knowledge in the classroom.

The "anything goes" sexual era on campus that faculty members may recall from their own undergrad years is now a relic of the past. Some students may object to classes that try to educate them on how to think or behave sexually. Controversial or explicit sex-ed classes have recently led to faculty firings, and colleges can expect controversies such as these to arise more often and lead to wider media coverage. Similarly, the definition of appropriate personal relationships between faculty and undergrads will narrow. Not only are Millennials themselves more sexually cautious than the prior two generations of college students, they have been raised in grades K through 12 with new rules rendering them less "touchable" than earlier generations of children. They will expect—and the public will insist—that a greater sense of restraint continues to be observed in college, both by fellow students and adults on campus.

8 | Confident

"In some ways they are as wholesome
and devoid of cynicism as the
generation that wore saddle shoes."

— *NEW YORK TIMES* (2000)

Confident

Far more than today's older generations, Millennials are inclined to assume that, as a group, they can meet any standard and beat any challenge. On the whole, the members of this generation feel less doubt—about the world or themselves—than young people used to feel. There's a new youth attitude that is gradually transforming into a strong collective assurance. According to a Bayer/Gallup "Facts of Science" survey, 84 percent believe someone in their own generation will become the next Bill Gates, 66 percent believe they personally know such a person, and one-quarter believe they actually are that person.

Whatever problems are facing their world, Millennials assume they can be fixed. At the same time, they accept that these solutions will take a substantial amount of planning, work, and sacrifice. They see their own generation as the key to addressing these problems. More than Boomers, and far more than Gen Xers at the same age, they like to apply their analytical skills to thinking through the long-term consequences of personal choices and acquired habits. This optimistic long-term thinking is being encouraged by parents, teachers, and leaders who want the next generation to be more positive about life.

The new youth confidence is widespread throughout the generation, but is especially prominent among young women. In high school, more girls than boys are applying for college. Of those, more are accepted—and, of those, more actually graduate. The flip side, clearly, is that fewer boys apply, fewer are accepted, and more drop out. In the years to come, colleges will face the challenge of helping Millennial men participate more in the sense of collective assurance and long-term mission that energizes their female peers.

Implications for Recruiting and Admissions

"Tell me you're proud of me" is a line from a circa-2000 anti-drug ad targeting child Millennials—a far cry from the "This is your brain; this is your brain on drugs" line in a famous early '90s anti-drug ad targeting Gen Xers. The recent shift toward more positive messages in youth-targeted ads exemplifies the attitude colleges should take in appealing to a new generation of applicants. The logic of the old Gen-X message was realism and damage control, to warn young people about the horrible things that would happen if they didn't do the right thing. The logic of the new Millennial-era message is optimism and positive reinforcement, to tell them about the great things that will happen if they do the right thing.

Rather than dwelling on how your college can provide a backstop and help students manage their problems, recruiting materials can describe an institution as a place where young people realize their dreams and where most students are capable of wonders. Today's high school students do not need to be reminded that success requires hard work, and that hard work does not necessarily lead to success. A better marketing concept is to show a college as a place upbeat and capable students can go to meet and work and develop lifelong friendships with other upbeat and capable students.

Recruiting and retaining Millennial men will pose a particular challenge to colleges in the coming years. The past decade has seen a steadily increasing advantage in the number of female over male college applicants, undergrads, and graduates. In 2005, 57 percent of all college freshmen were women, a proportion that has gradually risen from year to year since the 1950s, when barely one collegian in three was female. At some liberal arts colleges, and for African-American students nationwide, the female share is roughly 65 percent—very different from Boomer college days, when men greatly outnumbered women, and the minority gender shares were close to fifty-fifty.

Underlying this gender imbalance is a growing gap in academic achievement as measured by most current assessments. Men score as well as (or better than) women in pure aptitude tests, but by nearly every measure of applied effort women now come out on top. With all the new stress on teamwork and social skills, grading systems that favor steady over erratic performance and "zero tolerance" of what some might call typical boy behavior—combined with the usual late maturing of their gender—young Millennial males feel at a disadvantage against their female peers. By the time they leave high school, many develop an aversion to educators who (they think) regard them primarily as problems. Even bright and energetic young men often search desperately for alternatives (military service, construction, high-tech, business start-ups) to anything resembling more school.

To attract more young men, college recruiters must understand that their first challenge is to combat these perceptions. They need to demonstrate how the challenges and payoffs of their institution—everything from the intellectual excitement it offers to way it is assessed, from the character transformation it promises to the practical outcomes it delivers—is entirely unlike school as they have known it.

Millennial males will want to know that attendance at a particular college will equip them not just with a credential, but with a career. An effective strategy to attract and retain them will be to track the local economy, develop data that can prove that the knowledge given to students is relevant for practical employment, and offer them counseling, placement, and alumni networking programs to reinforce those outcomes. To a generation of males with record-low rates of employment before college, the message should be conveyed that their job histories—their demonstrated ability to earn real money by taking charge and getting tasks done—will be as valued in the admissions process as extra AP exams or internships in exotic locales.

Colleges can diversify their marketing by encouraging some male high school seniors who are unsure about what they want to do to take a year off and work, and then apply at age 19. They can also target those who have chosen to pursue other post-secondary options (like military service), but who might be willing to give college a try in their early twenties. Unskilled work that seems to pay relatively well at age 20 often doesn't look so appealing by age 25, when many young men figure out that, unlike in careers requiring an education, the pay for lower-skilled work will never get much higher. Colleges that are starting or expanding a distance-learning program should court these male "late bloomers," who—though unwilling to go on-campus at first—may well be attracted to trying college out on-line.

Implications for Campus Life

The "rah-rah" spirit of campus life recalled by today's oldest Americans is on track to return, updated for the new century. To the despair of faculty members who voiced counter-cultural dissent during their own college years, many Millennials will reveal what their edgier elders might deem "corny-cultural" values, but with a very modern twist. Rituals of recognition and celebration are fundamental in the lives of today's young people. Jostens, a leading producer of trophies, yearbooks, and class rings, has programs to celebrate the key moments in kids' lives as early as kindergarten. Today's collegians may find nothing inauthentic about college spirit in a modernized rebirth of pep rallies, awards ceremonies, school songs, proms, and the like. They will find in such activities a helpful release from the pressure to achieve and a cathartic expression of their own solidarity.

Once men are enrolled, colleges face a challenge in retaining them. One effective strategy is to develop a more male-friendly campus environment. This means getting male freshmen and sophomores more involved in campus spirit. According to the Chartwells 2006 College Student Survey, a higher share of men than women say that the "social" part of college is "extremely important"—including such activities as meeting new people, having fun, being part of a student body that shares values, and joining an alumni network. Not many colleges have been effective in tapping into this latent male desire to be joiners.

Many Millennial men enjoy group interaction that enables them to use technology and solve problems. Males are getting involved in Information Technology clubs, LAN parties, "'bot wars," computer-gaming tournaments, games that require puzzle-solving (virtual or real), and unconventional contests like decathlons or scavenger hunts. Unlike Gen-X students, who gravitated towards "survival" skills, destroying the enemy, and identifying winners

Gender Wars

The last three or four decades have witnessed a heated debate about how well each gender is performing in America's schools—and about what should be done to treat each gender fairly. Until the late '90s, the dominant view was that the educational system systematically disadvantages girls. Compared to boys, it was alleged, teachers were paying less attention to girls and expecting less of them; the curricula were designed to be more interesting to boys; and the exams overlooked many of the "soft" or consensual skills at which girls typically excelled. These biases were alleged to be key reasons why men of older generations were out-earning women in the workplace. The American Association of University Women issued a famous summary of this argument in its 1992 report, *How Schools Shortchange Girls*.

Later in the '90s, others began questioning this line of reasoning. If boys were so privileged, they asked, why were they so much more likely than girls to receive low grades, be categorized as disabled, claim they are bored or dislike school, drop out before graduating high school, and avoid or drop out of college? Moreover, the skeptics asked, why has the boy-girl gap on all of these counts gotten worse over time? While critics acknowledged that teachers were paying more attention to boys, they asserted that this attention was mostly disciplinary—and that, in fact, boys in grades K-12 were suffering under a feminized teaching style. This "boy backlash" was well articulated in 2000 by Christina Hoff Summers' book, *The War Against Boys*.

Few colleges have managed to stay out of this debate, since it touches on so many areas of collegiate policy. Should colleges change how they teach remedial subjects to reflect the disproportionate male presence in remedial classes? Does the fact that (according to surveys) women continue to focus less on future earnings handicap even the highest-achieving women in their careers? How can colleges induce men to be more active in campus life?

Most of all, colleges are wondering what if anything should be done about the growing numerical advantage of females on campus. Ever since the fall of 1979, when women first barely outnumbered men nationally among college undergrads, the gender margin has steadily widened throughout the Gen-X college era and, so far, into the Millennial era. The ratio now favors women, 57 to 43 percent—reflecting a "deficit" of over two million men. The ratio in graduate school is slightly more skewed, at 59 to 41 percent. The ratio among racial and ethnic minorities is more lopsided than among whites. Just over 65 percent of the total black college student body is female. Many liberal arts colleges, even while publicly adhering to the fairness-for-women argument, are worried that gender-blind admissions policies may soon push their female majorities toward an anti-male tipping point. Some, it is said, are employing a kind of "stealth affirmative action" to admit more males.

Behind the charges and countercharges, an expert consensus is emerging on a few basic facts. It is by now widely agreed that the two genders as a whole learn differently, for reasons that many say may have a biological basis since the differences appear so regularly across cultures. This difference shows up in achievement patterns by subject (for example, girls tending to excel more in verbal and reading tasks, boys more in spatial and math tasks). It also shows up in learning psychology: Girls more often learn well with extrinsic motivation and tend to do better on learning measures having a social or effort-related dimension (homework, class grades, school honors). Boys more often require intrinsic motivation and tend to do relatively better on pure aptitude tests (like the SAT, where males continue to outscore females on average, despite the large female advantage in GPAs).

Another big difference is that, along the spectrum of achievement, boys tend to be more dispersed or "spread out" around the average than girls. On the one hand, boys are much more likely to experience academic failure. They comprise 90 percent of discipline referrals, 80 percent of ADD or ADHD diagnoses, 75 percent of drop outs, 70 percent of students in special ed, and receive 65 percent of all D's and F's. On the other hand, boys outnumber girls among the very highest achievers. Not only do males get somewhat higher averages in such exams as the PSAT, SAT, GRE, GMAT, and MCAT, but among the top scorers on these exams (top ten percent, five percent, one percent), males outnumber females by progressively larger majorities. One can only speculate whether some of this greater "spread" might be biological, or might simply reflect boys' greater willingness to take risks in their behavior and lifestyle choices.

Our growing understanding of these gender differences may help to explain why changes in K-12 education during the Millennial era may have contributed to the widening of the gaps between boys and girls. The same reforms that have recently steered schools toward structure, regular exercises, quick feedback, tight behavior management, and grading that rewards consistency may have also created an environment in which boys find it harder to succeed—and which boys more than girls would like to avoid if at all possible. Achievement scores for both genders have risen, but perhaps at some cost in male enthusiasm. Today, boys today are less likely to encounter the sorts of teaching styles they find especially appealing—styles emphasizing invention, applied problem-solving, deferred feedback, and grading that rewards risk.

Colleges need to pay attention to gender. To attract and retain qualified males, they need to understand what best suits young men in the classroom and in campus life—and why they want college to be something other than the K-12 school they have known. To best serve their female student body, colleges may want to caution young women against becoming too fond of school (and the endless pursuit of higher honors and graduate degrees) without serious consideration of the real-life careers for which they are preparing. In-depth career counseling, or even a course on careers and labor markets, would be of great value to both genders of a generation whose members increasingly want to make long-term life plans. It would benefit the men by telling them what they really want to know (perhaps dissuading them from going elsewhere to learn it). It would benefit the women by telling them what they really need to know (and might otherwise never find out).

and losers, Millennial men prefer contests that are teamwork-oriented and (when possible) provide professional or academic recognition.

Implications for the Classroom

Millennials perceive greater dangers, and fewer rewards, in any attempt to be creatively different from their peers in the classroom. "Follow the rules, work really hard, don't mess up"—that's the new credo. One hears less talk about winning, standing out, or being unusually creative or imaginative.

Millennial women appear to be leading this trend as the more risk-averse collegiate gender, the ones more likely to do what they're "supposed to" and less likely to question where the collegiate award-ladder is taking them. Millennial males are just as ambitious, on the whole, but are less often convinced that college courses will help them achieve their goals. Colleges can encourage male students by restructuring courses to reflect their interests. Beyond emphasizing abstract ideas and theoretical thinking, some classes can offer learning that is more contextual and project oriented. In their effort to retain men, four-year liberal arts colleges in particular must recognize that they are in competition with technical institutes, business start-ups, the military, apprenticeships, and community colleges, all of which emphasize a more "hands-on" approach.

Compared with prior collegiate generations, today's students are less comfortable working independently. At the same time, they reveal a greater tendency toward consensus-building. Faced with a challenge, they are very quick to ask (or IM) each other for advice and support—and perhaps to seek a "safety in numbers" kind of consensus. This new youth conformity may be discomfiting, particularly to Boomer professors who recall a very different classroom environment in the 1960s or '70s. One often hears the lament that students are less willing than before to debate issues with each other or challenge a professor's point of view.

To tap into the latent creativity of Millennials, professors first need to understand how much today's students have been "taught to the test" through their K-12 years, and may be unfamiliar with taking intellectual risks. They then need to structure their instruction so that students who take risks and come up with the right approach end up helping their "team" and saving everyone from wasted time and effort. Channeled the right way, this generation's group orientation can turn from the problem into the solution.

Millennial risk aversion is worsened by grade inflation. When all smart students are presumed to get A's, a student can only lose by taking a risk with a creative paper that might not appeal to an opinionated professor or an experimental project that does not come to a neat conclusion. Studies have confirmed that grade inflation has been more pronounced at the more selective schools, and less so at state universities, prompting complaints that affluent students can, in effect, purchase higher grades by attending more expensive institutions. The recent trend has been to crack down on grade inflation, even at some schools that have previously avoided these reforms. Princeton now limits the number of A's in undergraduate courses to 35 percent or fewer.

A college may have difficulty counteracting grade inflation without going through a long period of demoralizing adjustment. To borrow an analogy from monetary currencies, a college may simply want to switch to a different currency. For example, the faculty could switch from a letter-based to a number-based grading system, or invent a "special honor" grade higher than an A to make the new A the equivalent of what a B or B+ used to be.

Honors programs are also affected by the Millennial trend toward risk aversion. The commitment to "go for honors," where that choice is available, will be more popular if the standards for achieving those honors are clear in advance. Many students will not want to risk spending lots of time and effort—and possibly even a bad grade—for an uncertain gain. Whether one speaks of low grades or high ones, honors degrees or honors fraternities, Millennials prefer to see a clear explanation of exactly what is expected of them.

9 | Team-Oriented

"We're seeing a huge cultural shift away from the word 'I' to the word 'We' in this new generation of young people coming in. And that's to be celebrated."

— GENERAL JAMES JONES, U.S. MARINE CORPS COMMANDANT (2002)

Team-Oriented

From pre-school through high school, from Barney and select soccer to school dress codes and collaborative learning, Millennials have been developing strong team instincts and tight peer bonds. No older person could visit a school classroom over the last several years without being impressed by the new emphasis on teamwork. At military academies, counselors are reporting a sharp drop in incoming recruits who say they want to "be the best" or "be number one" and a sharp rise in those who say they want to serve their group and be able to do what their team requires. From one generation to the next, the catch phrase has changed from "just do it" to "let's do it." Meanwhile, peer pressure is gaining a newly positive connotation. Social marketers now find that safety or anti-drug messages that tell teens to improve their behavior so as not to let a friend down often work better than messages that target a teenager's own self-interest.

As the first generation in history to grow up in a digital age, Millennials expect non-stop interaction with their peer group in ways that would have been unimaginable to previous generations of youth. Between morning classes, students can be seen on cell phones, keeping in close touch with friends on campus or back home. They use the Internet to stay in constant contact with large circles of friends and acquaintances via chat rooms, buddy lists, and networking tools. They use a variety of digital and mobile entertainment platforms to share their favorite bits of culture—including their own creations.

Implications for Recruiting and Admissions

College recruiters can to take advantage of the strong role of peers among Millennials. Military recruiters recognize how, along with family, peers are the dominant influencers of a young person's decision to enter the armed forces. Advertisers are discovering the same thing. For prior generations, the opinions of friends and classmates have always been important—but for Millennials, they are critical.

Millennials place a higher value than Gen Xers on going to the same college as their high school friends. Back in the 1960s, many Boomers preferred to go to colleges attended by no one they knew. Conformity may be the shadow side of the Millennial Generation, but it is undeniably a powerful motivator. As the appeal of "making it on your own" dwindles, recruiters can think anew about how teens influence each other in making life decisions.

Many colleges are already using enrollment management systems, designed to maximize overall student retention, that implicitly harness peer influence. Instead of focusing exclusively on prospects with the highest GPAs, for example, enrollment management software can focus on very good but not superior students (say, with 3.3 to 3.5 GPAs), from specific regions or with certain non-scholastic interests or achievements, as a way to build a more cohesive and loyal student body.

> ### Millennial Attitudes Toward Affirmative Action
>
> Asked nationally of 2006 freshman class:
> **"Affirmative action in college admissions should be abolished."**
> 47% agree "strongly" or "somewhat"
> (*The American Freshman*, UCLA, 2006)
>
> Asked nationally of college undergrads in 2004:
> **"I think college affirmative action programs should be abolished."**
> 50.4% agree
> (*College Student Survey*, Texas Tech University, 2004)
>
> Asked of sixteen hundred teens in on-line poll:
> **"Do you agree with using affirmative action as a factor in college admissions?"**
> 81% no
> 19% yes
> (*Teen People*, September 2001)

Millennial collegians (and high school students on campus visits) see racial diversity in a campus community as a hugely appealing part of the college experience. They believe it helps unlock something important and positive that their generation has to offer. Recruiters can advertise whatever ethnic diversity their institutions provide by highlighting it in a Millennial style, which means embracing a wide new range of racial definitions rather than pigeonholing races into fixed cultural or economic boxes. Millennials believe more in a "trans" racial than a "multi" racial society, an image better conveyed by blended pigments than white next to black, by dozens of races cooperating rather than two or three races pulling in different directions.

More than their parents at the same age, Millennials are bothered by preferential admissions quotas or formulas based on race. One reason may be that today's teens, aware of the growing and immigrant-boosted racial diversity among their peers, do not believe that simple yes-no categories can possibly match racial reality any more. Another reason may be the rapidly rising number of affluent nonwhite households and the high visibility of wealthy athletes and other celebrities of color—both of which erode, in teens' eyes, the old association between minority race and social disadvantage. For many Millennials, the biggest issues of social fairness hinge on whether someone comes from a poor or immigrant family or is of Arab descent, groups that do not usually benefit from affirmative action. Whatever the reason, preferential rules on race strike many of today's collegians as less about equal opportunity than simply about race *per se*. This sits uncomfortably with this generation's "fair play" ethic.

As social activism among Millennials grows in cohesion and effectiveness, it will increasingly target issues of class and income rather than gender or race. Collegiate efforts to reposition affirmative action as an income- rather than a race-based policy may meet with favor among prospective students. Well before high school graduation, Millennials are becoming aware of the widening gaps that separate families by income and, therefore, of the unequal struggle among parents to finance their children's education. Many Millennials wish they could do something constructive to help bridge these gaps. Students at Princeton are launching Zandigo, a web-based company that aims to financially democratize the college admissions process.

Colleges can appeal to Millennial recruits by presenting themselves as unifiers across economic class, bringing people together from every walk of life. In the Boomer collegiate era, institutions of higher education—including those with the highest tuitions and most selective admissions—were generally perceived to be social instruments for broadening opportunity and narrowing class differences. In the Millennial era, colleges are increasingly perceived to be accelerators of socioeconomic splintering, "Engines of Inequality," according to a recent report with that title published by the Education Trust. To cast a different tone, a college can emphasize how everyone is treated equally, what standards every student is expected to meet, and what money *cannot* buy on campus. This message will be sufficiently popular among incoming students to override the complaints of some Boomer and Gen-X parents who regard college as just another market transaction in which each family gets what it chooses.

Implications for Campus Life

College students used to view off-campus housing as a sign of their independence. Now many schools are opening up more on-campus housing as students welcome the opportunity to maintain stronger social connections. Many colleges are seeing a dramatic jump in the number of student clubs and organizations.

Millennials can build and belong to campus communities without having to gather in person as much as prior generations did. Today's college students engage in intensive digital interaction through blogs, computer and video games, cell phones, and on-line networking tools. Boomers often comment that technology has isolated too many young people from one another, but Millennials view technology more as a communal networking tool than as an enabler of solitary research and entertainment. A student who appears to be sitting alone in front of his computer may be playing interactive, web-based computer games with the girls down the hall (and perhaps young people in India too). Millennials are also using technology as a means of ad-hoc group creation. In a new phenomenon called "cell phone swarming," groups can gather instantly, without prior plans and without a single leader, through impromptu uncoordinated networking of text-messages and calls. Earlier generations of youth, by going in person to the town square or mall, had to congregate in order to communicate. Thanks to technology, this generation of youth can communicate in order to congregate.

As Millennials usher in a rebirth of college community, campus officials can take a cue from secondary school counselors and be mindful of loners. Surveys confirm that teenagers have become more dependent on relationships over the past decade. They value friendships more, spend less time alone, and pay more attention to peer opinion. This results in a more cliquish, rule-oriented social world—a world in which cooperation is prized, looking after your friends is priority number one, and being "nice" is esteemed. Yet it is also a world in which social outsiders—the bullied boy or the snubbed girl—can feel greater pain and be much harder to spot: Is that boy who's always in his room networking with peers electronically, or just sitting by himself?

One of the lessons of Columbine and the other multiple school shootings of the 1990s is that, amid this very social generation, those who don't fit in can, in extreme cases, become very dangerous. Some research suggests that this problem tends to be worse among more affluent youths, whose more frequent personal and financial help from parents can diminish their ability to develop support networks among their peers—or solve problems independently.

Millennials love group work, cooperative activities like volunteer service, and participating in something larger than the individual. This new youth attitude toward service can provide colleges with many opportunities to create a vibrant and exciting campus life. An unprecedented 83 percent of incoming freshmen in 2005 reported that they volunteered during their senior year of high school. The proportion who said it is "very likely" they will volunteer in college is also at an all-time high. For Boomers, community service was often an alternative to getting drafted to go to Vietnam. For Gen Xers, it was often a punishment for misbehavior. For Millennials, it's the norm—an expected part of anyone's educational experience. And, like many strong norms, the appeal is especially powerful among the elite. Teach for America, known as the "new Harvard" among post-graduate programs, accepts only one in five applicants. (The teachers they accept have an average SAT score of over thirteen hundred).

Student political participation within college communities will continue to intensify as Millennials flood college campuses. Millennials are voting in greater numbers. Student governments (and judiciaries) are assuming new importance on campus, especially where college administrators expand the students' authority over student rules, discipline, campus activities, and service. To this point, Millennial girls have dominated high school student governments and can be expected to do likewise in college.

Each year, as additional cohorts of Millennials enter college, self-segregating dorms, clubs, and eating areas could become less popular and more controversial—even repellent to many potential applicants. The Millennial focus on community building will also redefine race and ethnicity as campus issues. In the 1960s and '70s, college students reacted against the "melting-pot" homogeneity of the prevailing society by exploring and celebrating racial and ethnic difference. In the 1980s and '90s, immigration was rapidly on the rise, making Gen X the most immigrant generation born in the Twentieth Century. Back then, college students accepted a multicultural world view that tolerated, and at times even encouraged, racial and ethnic separation. Millennials, by contrast, are more often *second*-generation immigrants, which makes them more assimilation minded and more likely to focus on what people of different races have in common. Today's teens widely believe they handle race more constructively than older people and do not take well to being lectured to or chastised about it.

As issues of race and ethnicity become less divisive on campus, issues of income and wealth are becoming more so. Millennials understand that some students take advantage of resources from parents to enhance their college experience in very lavish ways, while others must take out loans, deliver pizzas, and ride on buses just to make ends meet. These differences make many collegians uncomfortable, including the affluent students themselves.

Alleviating class distinctions on campus is a difficult challenge, given the shift away from need-based aid and toward "legacy" admissions and early admissions (which favors applicants who don't need financial aid)—and given all of the less tangible advantages that come with family connections and expensive counselors. On today's campuses, students can take part in a variety of services that are increasingly differentiated by price, from dorm and food choices to participation in campus activities. Some students find it embarrassing to choose a meal plan that is markedly more downscale—or upscale—than that of their peers. Financial aid counselors should monitor the year-to-year financial circumstance of lower-income students to make sure that no student suffers a crushing work or debt load. The proliferation of cars is a very visible symbol of the widening economic gap between students, and colleges may want to even the playing field by imposing school-wide car limits, restricting parking, or replacing parking fines with community service requirements.

These issues could become increasingly important in Millennials' on-campus politics. To the extent Millennials feel trapped by this money problem, they may also assume a collective responsibility for solving it—in their campus communities as well as in society as a whole. Boomers' efforts to address issues of race and gender began on the campuses of the late 1960s. Millennials could soon do the same, in their own style, with issues of income and class. They may eventually organize major political and economic movements to deal with them, much in the way Boomers grew up in an era of sharp gender and race differences and later took major steps to narrow those differences.

Millennial on-campus campaigns are likely to include energetic advocacy on behalf of junior faculty and low-wage workers on campus or in the local community who complain about pay or working conditions. In time, some Millennial collegians may fuel a class-based agenda whose objectives may clash with their colleges' perceived need to keep raising tuition. As the Millennials pass through college propelling these and other political movements, some campus administrators may yearn for the good old days when collegians cared more about cultural or ethnic "awareness" and less about economic and political organizing.

Implications for the Classroom

Through their K-12 years, many Millennials have come to expect team teaching and team grading of group projects. College professors may discover that when they tap into this generation's team instincts, they can energize deeper commitment, more creativity, and better overall results. They can prepare them for a future workplace which, in most cases, will require people to work well with others.

More colleges are encouraging students (or, with freshmen, requiring students) to enroll in "learning communities," where two or more courses are team-taught with coordinated curricula and some student collaboration. Millennials are especially attracted to "living-learning communities," in which both the enrolled students and faculty live in the same dorm and can conveniently schedule intensive group study and discussion.

In any course, a challenge for faculty is to take advantage of team skills while encouraging each student to apply and develop his or her own efforts and skills. One strategy is to require students to perform independent assignments in a framework that requires them, in the end, to integrate all their work into some collaborative output. To grade each student on his or her performance, professors can adopt the same kinds of assessment methods that senior managers, clients, and customers will apply to these students when they enter the workplace. A work task isn't evaluated until it's completed and delivered, at which time all individuals who took part in it have their reputations on the line and will be asked to evaluate each other. In the role of teacher, a professor is in effect like a team supervisor ("Is there a better way to do this?")—but when grading, a professor becomes more like a client ("How good is it, in the final analysis?").

Accustomed to working together using interactive technologies, Millennials often regard a lectures-only course as a relic from another century. Instead of smothering their digital-age skills, professors can find ways to harness them. Doctoral students at the University of Texas San Antonio developed WebCT, a computer conferencing software tool that allows groups of students to work interactively from home through chat rooms and discussion groups. The University of Cincinnati renovated academic buildings to put in what they call "smart classrooms" with internet hookups, computers that play DVDs, and projectors that display documents. Professors at dozens of colleges across the country are "course casting"—putting their lectures on the internet (or on Apple iTunes) for students to download onto iPods for constant reference.

Boomer faculty may see potential problems in the use of technology in college-level learning. According to some professors, web casting or downloading classes can interfere with the critical personal dimension of teaching. In particular, many professors fear that if students can put lectures in their pocket or watch them late at night, then they might pay less attention in class—or not even come to class. Many faculty complain that students are using laptops in the classroom for IM chats and other distractions, while students contend that they are just taking notes and applying their own learning style to the material. Colleges can develop consistent protocols for the use of these technologies—for example, by suggesting that professors formally divide class time into note-taking and non-note-taking segments, or by giving students a pre-prepared set of notes and using class time for teaching and discussion.

The Millennial team ethic is prompting a shift in curricular choices and an apparent change in long-term career ambitions. In a sharp contrast with the Gen-X student era, today's collegians reveal a rising interest in permanent careers with stable businesses or public agencies and a declining interest in risky entrepreneurial start-ups. This will likely mean a greater interest in majors and degrees that can easily fit into conventional career definitions. In its 2006 annual survey of graduating college seniors, Universum Communications reported the highest-ever share who seek big-brand employers offering long-term career advancement, health and pension benefits, and a "balanced life." The desire for a career that makes a contribution to public life is also rising. When Universum asked the new grads to list their "ideal employers," government ranked right at the top. Among liberal arts majors, the top five were the U.S. Department of State, the Federal Bureau of Investigation, the Central Intelligence Agency, Walt Disney, and Google—in that order.

Interest in gender studies is likely to wane. For Millennials, feminism is a cause advanced by older generations more than by themselves. While they are grateful for prior advances, they see a need to update this original feminist agenda. The young Boomer challenge was to promote sexual independence by discarding social norms. The young Millennial challenge is to enable sexual *inter*dependence by updating (and re-energizing) social norms, including modesty, courtship, and monogamy. For Boomer women, marriage and kids were the norm; they had to struggle to pursue a career. For Millennial women, a career is the norm; they have to struggle to balance that with a fulfilling family life.

While continuing to be of interest, ethnic studies could change focus, with less student interest in the black-and-white issues (and dialogue building) that dominated the era in which many of these courses of study were launched. The cutting-edge fields will involve Latin American, Asian, and Islamic studies.

As Millennials become more invested in the nation's civic life, interest in the social sciences, applied sciences, and statistics will be likely to rise. This includes everything from macroeconomics, government, and political and military history to forensics, environmental technology, and civil engineering.

10 | Conventional

"Perhaps reacting to what might be
described as the excesses of their parents'
generation, teens today are decidedly
more traditional than their elders were,
in both lifestyles and attitudes."

— GEORGE GALLUP, JR., THE GALLUP ORGANIZATION (2002)

Conventional

When today's college freshmen were in third grade, the best-selling children's book of all time—*Harry Potter and the Sorcerer's Stone*—created a sensation in the nation's elementary schools. If ever there were an image reflecting the more ordered side of the Millennial Generation, it's the typical film shot of Harry in movie ads, showing a bright-eyed boy in glasses looking very proper in a uniform dress shirt and tie. This primness, and many other features of Harry's world, resonated with Millennial children in the late '90s. The learning environment in these books reflects, to some degree, how today's collegians struggle to excel and have fun in a very structured institutional environment.

Like Harry and his friends, today's collegians worry a lot about grades and exams and punishments and penalties. They often look up to a teaching faculty filled with wise but eccentric old spiritualists. Very few of them feel fundamentally alienated or oppressed. When they read the news, they realize they may someday have to band together to save the world—and, when they listen to their leaders, they hear little ambiguity about who the world's evil people are.

Polls show that most Millennials believe strongly in institutional trust, community standards, and personal responsibility. Few want to experiment with lifestyles or test the merits of cultural relativism. They like to focus on what they have in common, which helps explain why "social norming" campaigns (on substance abuse and sexual behavior) have worked better for them than they did for Gen Xers. Millennials cannot be described as "conservative" in the usual political or ideological definitions of that word. The term "conventional" fits them better—but in a modern context. Today's young people are not questing for a return to some bygone decade. Instead, they want to re-craft and update time-tested values to make them applicable for the needs of the Twenty-First Century.

Implications for Recruiting and Admissions

When making college decisions, Millennials tend to go with big brands, just as they do with clothes, cars, or credit cards. What are the top schools? What city is the campus hot spot? What big state university in which famous college town is getting the most buzz? In college, as in the rest of the marketplace, "brand" matters to Millennials and their parents. Colleges often build their brands and reputations around the sets of values that they believe they represent. Colleges are well aware that the students who are considering applying take a careful look at the various campus communities and evaluate how well they—and their values—will fit in.

College recruiters are encountering more young people who look upon themselves as good solid students with conventional values, want to succeed, and listen carefully to the advice of their parents and other adults. In 1971, only one in five freshmen said parents were a very important reason they were going to college. Today, two in five say this. Students are drawn to campuses that they perceive as being full of others who are much like themselves. This attitude is very different from what students wanted from campuses during the countercultural 1960s or the early dot-com 1980s and '90s.

Today, as in the 1930s, the era of the "regular" student is coming back. All recruiters should ask how young people with conventional values will view everything from the first campus visit to the personal interview and application process. At some campuses, many visiting high school students might get the impression that the school seeks out students who are odd or peculiar or unique. The challenge for recruiters is to convey that creativity and imagination are encouraged and rewarded—whether in class or in activities like music and drama—but also that the university has a faculty, curriculum, and deeply-held traditions that will resonate with the timeless and unchanging values of most student applicants and their parents.

Admission essay topics can be one key way a college can differentiate its values and its brand from those of others. What are the essays meant to reveal—conventional competence in composition, or bold originality of experience and expression? If a college creates the impression that it's looking mainly for the latter, many parents will be put off—and many Millennials, as they struggle to write about their "unique personal challenges," will question the whole premise of the exercise. What is wrong with being conventional, many may think, if it means trying to live up to a common and widely held standard of good behavior? Today's teens often associate excessive individualism with social dysfunction, or perhaps, as in Harry Potter's world, with inherent evil. Students might not want to go to a college whose student body seems to be dominated by unconventional people. Conversely, colleges can rise in reputation by appealing to young people who want to identify the new mainstream, meet its standard, and brand themselves for life as smart and capable members of that mainstream.

Implications for Campus Life

Millennials reveal a higher level of respect for institutions than collegians of the Boomer or Gen-X student eras, but with that respect comes high expectations. They count on adults to be exemplars—to practice what they teach. A professor or administrator who fails to live up to those expectations will lose their trust and may find it very difficult to earn it back. Millennials grew up in an era in which "zero tolerance" was the standard for misbehavior by youth, but not for misbehavior by celebrities and politicians, whose crimes and peccadilloes were repeatedly winked away. That double standard continues to rankle many Millennials. Administrators who fail to remove incompetent or unprepared professors—or any faculty member who engages in sexual harassment, uses drugs, or engages in fraudulent research—risk backlash from students and their parents.

In many ways, what today's parents remember of the sexual revolution is coming full circle. In the Boomer youth era, more went on than adults thought. In the Millennial era, less is going on. "It's funny," said Sarah Brown, director of the National Campaign to Prevent Teen Pregnancy, commenting on the continuing decline in the rates of teen pregnancy and abortion. "Never has anxiety been higher about bare midriffs and all-night raves. But kids are having less sex, and those who do are using contraceptives much more carefully."

Part of the adult misimpression about Millennials and sex arises from their frequent brashness when talking or writing about the subject. (One foreign journalist recently described American high school girls as "vulgar virgins.") Some college students have begun publishing explicit sex columns for campus papers even as these writers remain private about their own sexual experience. Had these columns appeared in the 1960s or '70s, they would have been an authentic part of a youth rebellion, out of step with the adult world. Today, these columns fit seamlessly into the adult celebrity circus that Millennials have grown up with—and, in many cases, are more designed to show how well they have mastered the genre than to say anything about their own feelings.

The same shift in generational experience applies to profanity. As a group, Millennial teens use more vulgar words than teens of past generations, but they are also more likely to borrow their expressions from what older people (mostly Gen Xers) have crafted for them. One analysis of teen profanity discovered that 80 percent of it was taken directly from adult performers in pop songs, sit-coms, or films. Many high school principals have observed that the quickest way to understand the improper or disruptive dress of a Millennial student is to meet the mom or dad in person. Back in the '60s, Boomers were more provocative than the world around them. Today's teens are less provocative.

At times, Millennials are chided for lack of politeness—from wearing flip-flops at the White House to not calling adults by surnames, from sending thank you notes by email rather than postal service, to using cell phones on trains or not saying sufficient pleases and thank yous. Again, it is necessary to ask: How many Boomer and Gen-X parents abide by these "manners" or have ever attempted to teach them to their kids? When older people do try to instruct young Millennials, nearly everyone agrees that they are much more receptive to learning than young Boomers ever were. In 2006, a conference was held in San Francisco to inquire into supposed problems with youth manners and mores. One wonders whether today's middle-aged San Franciscans

Where Have All the Streakers Gone?

American Pie 5: The Naked Mile, released in December of 2006 directly to DVD, features a group of graduating high school students who make plan to run sans-clothes in a college race called the "Naked Mile." Rarely has an exhausted movie franchise shown such bad timing in its hunt for a plot line that will connect with today's teens.

Yes, there actually is—or rather, was—a race called the Naked Mile. It happened annually at the University of Michigan. Started as a joke by the crew and lacrosse teams in 1986, this annual rite of spring was a Gen-X way to take an old Boomer prank—it was called "streaking" back in the '70s, a daring exhibitionist display by one fast-running loner—and turn it into a crowd phenomenon. By the late 1990s, the Naked Mile attracted between eight hundred and one thousand runners and more than twelve thousand onlookers on the streets of Ann Arbor.

After 1999, however, the popularity of the event suddenly ebbed. Students no longer felt like running, and if they did

they kept their boxers on. In 2002, only twenty runners showed up, and these were heavily surrounded by police. After 2004, the university and the city of Ann Arbor decided to cancel the event entirely—with practically no protest or dissent from the student body. Why the fade? The university and local law enforcement became stricter about enforcing rules and laws. More students began worrying about parents finding out, about blemishes on their record, and about having their bodies filmed and broadcast on the Internet. And many recent graduates now say that when they first witnessed the event as freshmen they were simply grossed out by the whole thing.

Over the past decade, young people have shown a new bent toward modesty that comes as a surprise to many older people, who believe much the opposite about them. Locker-room nudity has changed its generational aspect. In the 1970s, as today's fifty-somethings will recall, teenagers were far more likely than older people to

display their bodies in front of other people of the same gender. Today, the reverse is true—the result, in part, of the young generation's awareness of the number of cell phone cameras owned by their peers. They know, even if their professors might not, that an incautious moment and quick camera click can get a person on You-Tube.

To be sure, Millennials have absorbed the messages of the popular culture that surrounds them, including scantily-clad celebrities and explicit sexuality. But unlike Boomers or Gen Xers at the same age, they have grown up viewing edgy cultural elements as an accepted adult norm—not as their own youth rebellion. Today, the most explicit elements of pop culture tend to originate not with 16-year-olds, but with 35-year-olds—or even 55-year-olds. Today's young people take part in the prevailing edginess of the culture, but rather than stepping it up to the next level, they often rebel by stepping it down a notch, particularly in the presence of adults.

remember what their own manners and mores looked like, in the eyes of older people, back in their own Summer of Love youth.

Among themselves, Millennials are crafting new norms of manners and politeness, which they follow more strictly than older people realize. Some things that nearly all Millennials regard as rude—such as smoking around nonsmokers, getting angry when talking politics, or failing to share credit with co-workers—many older people consider acceptable behavior. Like other generations, Millennial collegians make the most out of being young, and that includes sex and slang—but unlike other generations, they will take the cues and follow the rules of older adults, as long as those cues and rules do not involve double standards. If college administrators or faculty advisors would like to tone down a sex column in a college paper or set language rules for a college radio station, Millennials might grumble a little at first but are likely to oblige in the end—as long as the same rules apply to what professors say in classrooms and write in academic journals. Unlike twenty or (especially) forty years ago, institution-wide security measures, or disciplinary crackdowns applied evenly to people of all ages, can be more controversial among older faculty members than among younger students.

Millennials are used to living in a rule-bound world. More than Boomers and Gen Xers at the same age, they are comfortable with "zero tolerance" for even minor infractions. Today's teens are somewhat more inclined than prior generations to report such infractions—and, when asked, are more likely to say that enforcement does not go far enough. When a student at Rocky Mountain College told an administrator that anyone parking illegally on campus should be expelled from school, the official commented, "Ten years ago, if you parked *legally* you were ostracized." Many Millennials willingly participate in student juries, which they often recall from their high school days.

On the whole, Millennials are better followers than Boomer or Gen-X collegians used to be. They are a generation willing to be led, whether by an administration seeking to impose new dress codes, by junior faculty and support staff seeking higher pay, or by off-campus organizers promoting any number of causes. With youth allegiance more available to adult leadership than was true in prior decades, some campuses may see major power plays among those competing to lead them. Much the same is likely to happen in national politics.

Implications for the Classroom

To be conventional is to aspire to balance and proportion in one's life—and this is changing what and how young people want to learn. According to a recent MIT admissions report, Millennial students are less likely to pursue one subject intensively and more likely to spread their time and their talents among numerous subjects and activities. Rather than distinguishing themselves with a unique course of study, they prefer to spend more time mastering a common set of skills and a common body of knowledge. Perhaps responding to this new student mindset, a rising number of schools are requiring all incoming freshmen to learn works of classical literature, books that were largely displaced in the '70s to make room for a broader array of less traditional subjects. Columbia University's great books curriculum remains more popular than ever with students. In 2005, George Washington University began requiring all freshmen to take a writing course. Millennials are drawn to the idea that there is a timeless body of knowledge that everyone should know—and can learn together.

During their college years, young Boomers believed that no one was telling "the truth" in America—and they felt it was their duty to pronounce it. Today, Millennials assume that everyone in America has their own "truth" to tell, leaving it to young people to impose order on the resulting hurricane of information, interpretation, and assertion. In this context, what is important about a history paper, customized CD, or community service web site is less its originality than its usefulness in simplifying the world and making life more manageable.

This Millennial agenda will attract plenty of complaints from middle-aged people of a self-professed "creative" bent—including many academics. In the torrent of responses to David Brooks' April 2001 *Atlantic* cover story, "The Organization Kid," a number of readers pelted the first Millennial collegians with descriptors like robotic, sheep, conformist, mechanical, eunuchs, shallow, and so on—comments written by Boomers and Gen Xers who came of age when, in their recollection, youthful prophets made of truer stuff strode the earth. Yet while the Boomer style of radicalism and Gen-X style of ironic detachment are aging right along with them, Millennials are developing their own style. Demonstrations against the war in Iraq have been populated more by the middle-aged teachers and parents of young soldiers than by young people themselves, a stunning age-reversal since the Vietnam War.

This has all the ingredients of a new generation gap, on campus and elsewhere. Boomers are no longer young activists. Millennials now have to fill that role. Just like Boomer parents, Boomer faculty may struggle a little as they learn to "let go." Many of today's collegians bristle at professors who condescend to them, or who lay claim to greater idealism or seriousness, or who cannot set aside old crusades that young collegians may regard as irrelevant. In the emerging Millennial mindset, it seems useless to be an "original" no one will imitate—or a leader no one will follow. Professors can challenge these assumptions, but they also need to be mindful of the generational experience that has made them so pronounced.

Highly politicized Boomer faculty members are starting to clash with Millennial students who value professionalism over passion. In the Chartwells 2006 Student Survey, 37 percent of Millennials said they are concerned about "too much political bias" in what professors teach. Students at the University of Texas posted a public list of professors they consider too politicized. Whatever teachers believe, these students want them to keep it out of the classroom. The proliferation of such lists and of professor-rating web sites has raised a backlash among many college faculties. Conflicts between Millennials and their Boomer professors will grow to the extent professors elevate their accountability to conscience and principle over their accountability to students and community norms.

In determining course content and leading class discussions, professors need to keep in mind that the various causes of the 1960s are as chronologically distant from today's Millennials as World War I and Prohibition were to Boomers when they were in college. Professors who envision Millennials as instruments for completing their unfinished societal agendas may come away disappointed, frustrated, and deeply critical of these new youth for the "lessons" they have supposedly "forgotten"—when in fact the real lesson of history is that generations, like time itself, must always move on.

11 | Pressured

"When I graduated from high school in 1994, we could take classes for enjoyment and not worry about how it would look on a transcript. Today, many kids can't take classes like music, photography, journalism, or yearbook because they fear they will fall behind in class rank…. If I were in high school now, and I had to compete with this pool of students, there is no way I would be able to keep up."

— ALEXANDRA ROBBINS, AUTHOR OF *THE OVERACHIEVERS* (2006)

Pressured

There's a new "arms race" among today's teens. It's called: "Getting Into College." According to recent surveys, the two challenges that worry teenagers the most these days are grades and college admissions. Four times as many high school students worry about getting good grades than about pressures to have sex or take drugs, and six times as many complain that they don't get enough sleep.

Millennials are feeling academic stress in ways Boomers and Gen Xers could not have imagined at the same age. Employers are asking to see high school transcripts, test scores, and attendance records. Grades have become more significant than ever. More homework is being assigned in the younger grades. Recess and physical education are disappearing and class periods are lengthening. Nervous students are turning to a rapidly expanding network of tutoring companies. In 1993, 577,000 students in grades 9 and 10 took the PSAT—a number that jumped to 990,000 in 2001 and 1.3 million in 2005.

All this pressure has led to an intense new emphasis on preparation and planning. Unlike Gen Xers, who excelled at improvisation and at tackling short-term problems, many Millennials have five- or ten-year time horizons. Millennials see too many adults around them—Gen Xers and Boomers alike—whose life-sequences lack order and coherence. Maybe too many options at age 21 can lead to too many roommates at age 32. And why didn't Dad start worrying about his retirement income *before* age 55?

This experience leads many Millennials to an intense desire for security, reliability—and, above all, balance—in life's arrangements. By 68 to 8 percent,

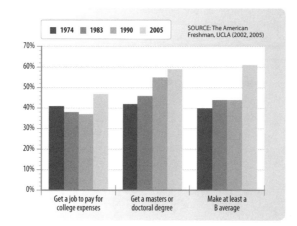

Figure 22 ▶

National U.S.
Freshmen Survey,
Expectations
for College

according to the Chart-wells 2006 Student Survey, Millennials say that a very or extremely important reason to go to college is "to become a more well-rounded person." Surrounded by adults with chaotic work lives (due to self-employment, contract-ing, and rapid job turnover), Millennials are far more interested than Gen Xers in institutions, including colleges, that can enhance job and life stability.

Implications for Recruiting and Admissions

Getting into college is more stressful than it used to be. Many colleges have noted the growing number of applicants who have geared their lives toward getting into "the right college," from the time they were in elementary school. As more Millennials follow this plan, admissions decisions will become tougher and more competitive—further fueling the cycle of pressure. In addition, more students are applying to larger numbers of colleges. At some high-pressure high schools, students apply to as many as twenty or even thirty colleges apiece. The large size of this generation and the rising number of students achieving good grades, graduating, and going on to college will only increase the competitive stress.

Millennials can flourish under lots of pressure. Far more than students of other eras, they have grown used to it. What many Millennials desire, and what they are competing most heavily over, is admission into the most intense aca-demic environments, where the high stress will continue. What demoralizes them is not pressure *per se*, but rather situations in which their best effort under pressure does not ensure success. What haunts them is uncertainty and risk—not knowing what the professor wants or what will be on the exam, having no idea how well they may be doing in a course or program, or not knowing where their major or degree will lead. Recruiters can help by reassuring prospective students and their parents that their college will let no one get lost, offer continuous feedback, and do its best to put every student on a sound professional or academic career path. The message should be: Yes, students work hard here, but we help make sure all of their hard work will pay off.

There is such a thing as too much pressure, of course, and Millennials will be wary of an unrelieved emphasis on achievement. A college's recruitment literature can emphasize the distinctive things students do to relax. Many colleges now have "student wellness" committees that organize study breaks and student activities. Swarthmore College keeps a croquet set in its library collection for students to check out and use on the library lawn. College tours can include these details to show prospective students how they can lead balanced lives on campus even while pursuing a strenuous college curriculum.

Colleges can help shield students from parental intrusions, which often add fuel to the pressure felt by today's collegians. This can begin with the college application process, where colleges can restrain parents from taking too active a role. Cheating on application essays is impossible to measure—and probably widespread. It can range from mom and dad helping out with punctuation to the hiring of professional wordsmiths. Admissions staff can address this in part by holding sessions without parents present, and by maintaining ongoing communication directly with applicants. Usually, these actions will be welcomed by the students, if not the parents.

In this sense, a college education can be exactly what Millennials need: the opportunity to break away from a constantly scrutinized, heavily protected childhood and to enter into a more self-directed adulthood. Colleges can do many young people a favor by helping them acquire not only the bottom lines of achievement, but also—in the absence of constant parental help—the values, habits, and skills that will craft them into the kind of adults they want to be.

Implications for Campus Life

While Millennials accept academic challenges and may thrive under pressure, they are prone to suffering occasional periods of burnout. Many have never learned to create a suitable balance between work and play. On today's campuses, though "work-life balance" is a goal widely praised by both students and deans, it is far less often achieved. According to the UCLA American Freshman survey, a record share of new students report feeling so "overwhelmed" that they have sought counseling. Some students see this as a problem and want to fix it. Others forge on, in ways older people may find impressive and oppressive, sometimes pleasing but other times disturbing.

Sleep deficit disorders have become a serious recent problem among high school and college-aged Millennials. The contributing causes reflect the new 24/7 habits of today's young people—from a daily habit of irregular meals and hours (often learned from workaholic parents), to over-scheduling (with "down time" coming at the expense of sleep), to inadequate physical exercise among those who do not excel in sports. Colleges have difficulty combating this, and many students might not want them to take the measures that may be required to alter the students' daily regimens. Colleges can reduce the number of early morning classes and offer a more diverse range of physical activities, including intramural sports for students who are not trained athletes (and who therefore need the physical activity the most).

One of the best ways to relieve Millennials' stress levels while improving their fitness is to encourage physical activities that require no formal time commitment. A college can organize unconventional sporting events like kickball or flag-football tournaments and support club-sports like rugby and ultimate frisbee. Kenyon College's intramural sports program offers tournaments and activities ranging from wiffle ball to three-on-three basketball. Unconventional sports such as these will help Millennials come to see physical activity as a lifestyle rather than an elite competition.

Getting Millennials to exercise more is best done by helping them restructure their lives, not necessarily by building conventional gyms of the kind that have so appealed to Boomers and Gen Xers, with dozens of of individual exercise "stations." Many Millennials prefer their exercise programs to be more socially oriented—for example, a college might lend students pedometers in events where they "walk for a cause" around campus, with sponsors donating money depending on the number of steps taken. That familiar Boomer health mantra,

"It's not the destination, it's the journey," strikes younger ears as old fashioned. Millennials prefer not to try anything unless they know the destination.

Extracurricular activities outside sports can be among the best stress relievers, from music and drama to publications and community volunteering. Students can obsess (and lose sleep) over these too, so the challenge for colleges will be to prompt students to dabble in and explore new activities without the pressure of full commitment or the constant need to excel. Finally, stress-free "chill zones" on campus can provide collegians with quiet, out-of-the-way places where they can gather to play high-tech video games, low-tech ping pong, or just sit on cushy couches and watch movies in small groups. Such zones should be available as close to 24/7 as possible.

Implications for the Classroom

Any discussion of pressure soon leads to the issue of cheating. Some professors believe that student cheating on formal exams has become vastly more commonplace today than a generation or two ago. No one in fact knows whether this is true. The scant research that does exist (of self-reported cheating by college students as far back as 1963) is ambiguous. According to one recent Gallup report, a steadily *declining* share of 13- to 17-year-olds has been answering "yes" to the question, "Have you yourself ever cheated on a test or exam?"—from 66 percent in 1981 to 44 percent in 2001.

With Millennials, the key cheating issue is not formal exam behavior, but the use of shared or copied information in research and writing. In this digital age the rules are changing, and neither Millennials nor their educators have been able to keep up. The difficulty stems in part from the group-oriented changes in pedagogy in K-12 schools, with more collaborative projects, take-home essays, and open-ended problem-solving.

Habituated to this kind of learning experience, today's college freshman may be confused about what kind of outside help is allowable—from parents willing to help a bit with the occasional college paper, to on-line digital googling and copying, to trading and remixing MP3 music files. These newly available technologies are blurring the distinction between what's original and what's not, complicating the very definition of cheating.

A special challenge in educating today's collegians is therefore to instill a clear understanding of where originality and plagiarism begin and end—a challenge that in the current cultural and technological environment will require considerable re-thinking. Some colleges have issued multi-page memos explaining "allowed" versus "dis-allowed" practices to students. Other colleges are requiring freshmen take special web seminars or sign "integrity contracts." Still other colleges are inaugurating or reviving honor codes, like Duke's requirement that students enforce a "community standard" for academic honesty. Honor codes work well with Millennials, as long as the same rules are imposed on faculty as on students.

Course by course, each professor needs to think through a strategy. Some lean toward proctored exams. Others go hi-tech and enlist on-line text screeners to catch malefactors. In 2005, Secure Computing found 780 web sites dedicated to on-line plagiarism, a ten percent increase from the year before. Younger, tech-savvy professors—who are tuned in to Millennials' digital mindset—are a great resource for advising more senior faculty on how best to cope. One good approach may be to supplement standard paper submissions with personal, team, or interactive presentations in which students must be prepared to think and respond on the spot.

The desire to live up to expectations—of adults, parents, oneself—is a powerful Millennial urge. In 2006, in a story that received extensive news coverage, a 17-year-old Harvard freshman published a wildly successful novel while taking a full course load. The publisher withdrew the book when it was discovered that passages had been copied from another author's work (the freshman insisted that the copying was "unconscious"). Many may have gained the impression that the author was just another reckless teenager who could not care less about the rules of the system, but a closer look shows a much more typically Millennial problem. This was an ambitious, straight-A, polish-the-teacher's-apple young woman with workaholic immigrant parents. She was so highly programmed to please her family and her publishers that personal originality seemed far less important than producing a universally admired product.

To combat plagiarism in the new digital era, colleges need to keep a broad sense of generational perspective. Overall, Millennials are focused less on the learning experience *per se* and more on the bottom-line test result. From their perspective, there is no clear distinction between traditional notions of exam cheating and modern notions of information "morphing." Many may see nothing wrong with simply rearranging, in a report or paper, a thought that someone else has expressed with elegance, especially if a student is merely employing devices used commonly in business, government, the media—or by professors in their own research. Millennials are less likely to feel the Boomer quest to come up something never before thought or said. Their major challenge is rather to sort, simplify, and synthesize knowledge in an information-overload world. As a result, they are more accepting of imitation, simulation, and condensation than Boomers were in their youth.

The entertainment industry is confronting this even more directly than universities. In the pop culture, Millennials are encountering more remakes of old songs and movies, more infotainment and advertorials that efface the identity of the author, and more teen willingness to download, alter, and share whatever sounds and sights please them. New digital and mobile technologies enable them to interact with their pop culture far more than any generation in history. They care less about who the original artist was, and more about how to access it, interact with it, change it, and spread it around.

In college classrooms—as in Hollywood board rooms—older generations are learning that, to keep young people from "cheating" as older people define the word, you have to meet them on their own terms.

12 | Achieving

"Once, summer for teenagers meant a season of menial jobs and lazy days at the local pool….Driven largely by increased competition to get into elite colleges and universities, teenagers are [now] jumping from demanding school-year commitments into equally challenging summer activities."

— *NEW YORK TIMES* (2006)

Achieving

Every year, the highest-achieving Millennials astound older Americans by showing off their academic prowess. In the Twentieth Century, the National Spelling Bee could be won with words like *knack* (1932), *therapy* (1940), *vouchsafe* (1973), or *lyceum* (1992). Consider the 6 winning words of the new millennium: tongue twisters like *succedaneum, prospicience, pococurante, autochthonous, appoggiatura*, or (the 2006 winner) *ursprache*.

Admissions officers at the nation's upper-ranking colleges are broadly reporting a recent rise in the qualifications of incoming freshmen. They admit that they are turning away vast numbers of applicants they could have admitted ten or fifteen years ago.

A much higher share of Millennial teens say they aspire to post-secondary education than the teens of any prior generation. Over seven in ten of today's high school students say they are aiming for a four-year college degree, and solid majorities of all races and ethnicities agree that a college degree confers "respect." According to the Chartwells 2006 Student Survey, they overwhelmingly say (by a ten to one margin) that having a college degree is "more important" for them than it was for their parents. By equal margins, they also say that college is "more academically challenging" and that the application process is "more stressful." Many teens who today want degrees may in time discover they lack the motivation, education, or money necessary to get them. Even so, this generation as a whole will be more inclined to let their best and brightest set the cultural tone than Boomers or Gen Xers were in their own youths.

Academics are hardly the whole picture. When you add their harder-to-measure but equally important accomplishments outside the classroom, the Millennial bottom line is very impressive. Student productions in music, theater, sports, publications, student government, student clubs, and community service are getting better every year.

Today's teens know this. They have a high regard for their own generation, which they see as a powerhouse full of high achievers, no matter what some politicians or op-ed writers might say about them. Day to day, this is less a matter of glowing pride than a constant source of personal pressure. One explanation for the continual improvement in behavior and risk avoidance of today's teenagers is their anxiety not to fall behind all of their achievement-minded peers.

Implications for Recruiting and Admissions

Colleges at every level all across America are reporting a rise in the quality of applicants and recruits. This is very good news for admissions offices, who might be forgiven their exuberance at basking in the success of their recent recruitment efforts. When so many colleges report the same result, the conclusion is clear: The new pool of students, not the new recruitment strategies, is making the difference. According to reports from admissions officers at top colleges, there are now enough high-achieving high school students to fill two or three Ivy Leagues and still send out rejection notices to plenty of qualified students.

For institutions of higher education, the implications are double-edged. Now is an opportune time for any college to raise its overall academic standing. But this also means that competition between admissions offices will rise as more and more colleges find this out. The college that does not rise will, in effect, be regarded as falling behind its traditional rivals.

To move up a notch, colleges should trumpet more than just academics. Millennials want to participate in a strong and diverse community life, and many are achieving highly in many extracurricular areas. In recruiting pitches, colleges can tout their infrastructure for student activities, especially for first- and second-year students. Many graduating high school seniors will have greatly enjoyed their leadership roles in the arts or publications or student

The Future of Early Decision

Though "early decision" admissions options date back decades—one of the first "early" plans was instituted by the University of Virginia in 1960—it was not until the late-1990s that these options became widespread. The most selective colleges led the way. According to NACAC's 1999 Admission Trends Survey, 27 percent of responding colleges (and disproportionately the elite colleges) offered early decision plans in that year. In many of these colleges, over half of the freshman class for the fall of 1999 was admitted via early decision or "early action" (a similar program that does not require accepted students to enroll).

Starting with the high school seniors of 2000—the first Millennials—some colleges, counselors, and parents began speaking out against early decision. In 2006, Harvard and Princeton announced that they would no longer admit any of their applicants early, though it is not yet clear whether other colleges are ready to follow their example. If anything, the early admissions movement is still advancing, with the proliferation of such new options as "instant decision," "fast-track applications," and "early decision two."

From the perspective of both colleges and Millennial applicants, early decision programs present a number of advantages and disadvantages.

In Favor of Early Decision:

- **Administrative advantages.** Spreading out the admissions process over more of the school year gives college admissions and financial aid officials more time to give individual attention to students.
- **Enrollment management.** Early admissions gives colleges more control over the composition of their incoming classes. Colleges can reduce the uncertainty of the size of each class and admit students for whom they are a clear first choice, not a backup to somewhere else.
- **Early peace of mind.** Millennials tend to want to plan ahead. Early decision gives students a chance to make their college choice ahead of time

and resolve everything early, thereby reducing the stress of their senior year.
- **Simplification.** Growing up in a world of complicated choices, many Millennials have the urge to simplify. With early decision, they can streamline their college choices and pick the one special school that is right for them.

Against Early Decision:

- **Financial inequalities.** Early decision favors students from wealthy families over those from middle- or low-income families. In particular, "binding" programs (those that require admitted students to attend) are not often feasible for applicants who will require significant financial aid, since they prevent applicants from shopping for affordable colleges and weaken their position for financial bargaining. Early decision therefore gives an advantage to applicants who are able to pay the full cost of tuition, especially children of wealthy alumni. Over time, given the Millennial sensitivity to issues of economic inequality, students will increasingly perceive this as a problem.
- **Shifting the bargaining advantage from student to college.** Viewed as a contract, early decision reverses the usual order of "offer" and "acceptance." In the normal spring admissions process, colleges make a binding offer, and then students have about a month to accept. In early decision, students

make a binding offer, and then colleges have a month or two to accept—and, if the offer is rejected, a student must often scramble to submit spring applications ahead of January deadlines.
- **Accelerated workload.** By pushing up the students' application deadline two months, early decision requires students to make college trips, take standardized tests, and write college essays over a shorter period of time. The rush to complete applications early can increase the stress on high school juniors and seniors.
- **Senior slump.** High school teachers complain that early-admitted students become less serious about schoolwork in the spring semester of the senior year, and that a split in morale can arise between those students whose college decisions are settled and those who are still uncertain.

In the Millennial college era—with intrusive parents and highly ambitious applicants, all under a media glare—every aspect of the college admissions process will be the focus of growing controversy and reform. Aspects of early decision are so appealing to Millennials that some form of this "fast track" process will likely endure. However, other aspects are problematic enough that colleges can expect the debate to continue, possibly ending in a dramatic reworking of how these programs operate.

government, and they will not want to wait until their junior or senior year of college to feel the same sense of participation and accomplishment.

With eyes on the annual *U. S. News & World Report* "yield" rankings, many colleges are pushing applicants to make binding "early decision" commitments at the start of senior year. Likewise, with eyes on their average SAT rankings, many private colleges are offering tuition cash-back discounts (alias "scholarships") to students with scores above a certain level.

At the same time, colleges do not want to recruit bright students who have a high probability of transferring out the next year. This is one reason why some of the smartest schools are explicitly focusing on a less elite clientele, rejecting applicants who are obviously looking upon them as a "safety" school. Instead, they are seeking students of an appropriate ability level and offering these recruits the biggest incentives to enroll. This can help a college to achieve a more durable community and a higher ratio of graduations.

Implications for Campus Life

Mirroring what has been happening in high schools recently, Millennial collegians will engage robustly in all kinds of extracurricular activities. The Gen-X collegiate era was marked by substantial construction of athletic facilities. Colleges would now do well to build other extracurricular infrastructure to match: art studios, meeting rooms, student offices, theaters, music halls, and more. These can be numerous rather than large, and preferably with cutting-edge technology.

Unlike the counter-cultural Boomers at their age, Millennials want to integrate themselves into the professional mainstream of their chosen careers, including their college extracurriculars. Some of today's college newspapers are almost indistinguishable from professional publications, and the short films and TV series produced by college students (and often broadcast on the Internet) can be of very high quality as well. Millennials do not want their activities to be ignored by other people and relegated to some "youth" space that no one ever will see. They believe, with some justification, that they are ready to perform successfully within the framework of today's dominant culture and institutions.

To connect with each other often and to arrive at a campus-wide (or even nationwide) consensus, Millennials will not need big physical structures. With fiberoptic cables in place, they will be able to set up a virtual forum of any size very quickly. A majority (57 percent) of teenagers who use the internet are also "content creators," who have put together a blog or a webpage, reworked on-line content to create new products, or posted original media on-line. Millennials themselves often pioneer the most popular on-line networking tools used by their own generation. In 2004, a Harvard undergraduate created "The Facebook," which has since grown into an immensely popular social-networking Mecca that connects students from over two thousand colleges nationwide. A student at Brown created the "Daily Jolt," a network of student-run college web sites where students communicate about life at their college through active discussion forums and postings on campus events. Communication technology will continue to flourish, driven by Millennial achievement. Schools need to provide collegians with the tools, and then let them go to work.

With all the new emphasis on achievement inside and outside the class-room, many Millennials push themselves relentlessly to get a performance edge. Athletes study the details of their nutrition and weight training, musicians compete for the best tutors, and—in remarkable twist on the '60s—large numbers of students are turning to "smart drugs" to help with papers and exams.

Where Boomers and Gen Xers once used drugs to drop out and misbehave, Millennials are using them to plug in and excel. The past few years have seen an explosion in the number of youths using drugs like Ritalin, Adderall, and Provigil to enhance their concentration and academic performance. One of every ten students in grades 7 to 12 is using these kinds of stimulants without a prescription. Half of these students are using the drugs not to get high, but to "help me with my problems" or "to help me with specific tasks," motivations that are becoming more important. Colleges can expect smart drugs to spread rapidly within their student bodies in the years to come. Counselors and health staff can warn students about the dangers and learn to identify those most at risk of dangerous abuse. As Richard Restak, President of the American

Neuropsychiatric Association commented, these "drug users may be at the top of the class, instead of the ones hanging around the corners."

Implications for the Classroom

More than the Boomers and Gen Xers who preceded them in college, Millennials enjoy grand challenges. Workplace surveys confirm that Millennials prefer tasks in which they, and the world, can measure their objective progress. They see their biggest advantages in technology, the economy, and the social sciences—rather than in religion or the arts. The physical and behavioral sciences can be expected to show the same kind of dynamism and innovation in the coming years that the humanities experienced during the Boomer student era and business and the arts did during the Gen-X student era.

In a reversal from the Gen-X student era, Millennials and their parents are accustomed to high academic standards, intense amounts of schoolwork, and strong internal and external pressure to overcome challenges. Students, parents, and public officials increasingly want higher academic standards, smaller classes, clearer grading practices, and a new Millennial-era mixture of traditional values with cutting-edge technology.

To get Millennials fully energized about higher education, it helps to spell out a clear goal, define an objective measure of success, explain possible strategies, structure their work in teams, and offer frequent feedback on their progress.

Older professors (Boomers especially) sometimes complain that many of today's students are so accustomed to quick turnaround assignments and a multitasking work style that big projects can overwhelm them. Having grown up feeling constant pressure to accomplish a multitude of discrete tasks, Millennials have developed great skill at turning rapidly from one problem to the next with more industry than reflection. This can make it hard for students to focus at length on an obscure text or persevere at length on a difficult math problem. Colleges can help by pushing Millennials, step-by-step, into low-pressure immersive environments. This may include two-hour presentation and discussion seminars with no laptops allowed, optional credit problems that require students to apply their learning in new ways, or tutorials in which professors explain step-by-step how to undertake large research projects or solve complex analytical problems.

Putting Generations to the Personality Test

Two sets of medical students, admitted into Northeastern Ohio University's College of Medicine in 1989 to 1994 and in 2000 to 2004, were given the same sixteen-factor personality test shortly after their arrival. The results were then sorted into three groups by birth cohort: those born from 1965 to 1975 ("Gen-X"); those born from 1976 to 1980 ("Cuspers"); and those born after 1980 ("Millennials").

Among the findings, as published by Nicole J Borges et al. in "Comparing Millennial and Generation X Medical Students at One Medical School" in *Academic Medicine* (vol. 81, no. 6; June 2006), are the following:

Millennials scored higher in...	Gen Xers scored higher in...	"Cuspers"...
■ emotional stability ■ perfectionism ■ rule orientation	■ risk taking ■ pragmatism ■ self-reliance	showed some of the traits of both generational neighbors.

In class, technology is a dimension colleges can integrate into every subject. Some faculty members may need remedial tech-ed just to come up to the minimal level that students will expect. Professors can teach students about the limitations of Internet research, especially the danger of unreliable sources and the absence of reliable sources that have not yet been digitized. As a generation, Millennials expect to eventually succeed in overcoming most of these limitations.

In classrooms and in extracurricular activities, high-achieving Millennials will expect to create products that compete actively with "real world" professional products. Over the last decade, large research universities increasingly find themselves owners of valuable patents and venture-partners in profitable research firms that give Millennials the opportunity to take on professionals roles before they graduate. More than a dozen schools that offer bachelor's degrees in music industry have recently launched their own student-run record labels, allowing students to create professional-level media products as part of their undergraduate coursework. Colleges that want to boost their reputations with ambitious students can find new ways to support student efforts to create professional-level products in a variety of academic fields.

In the spring of 2006, protestors gathered in cities all across America, rallying for the rights of undocumented immigrants to become U.S. citizens. Much of the organizing behind these protests was done by young Hispanics—often U.S.-born citizens, the children of immigrants—who startled the nation with how skillfully they mobilized their communities to action.

Far from the wild, rebellious "Hell No, We Won't Go!" demonstrations of the 1960s, which were calls for civic refusal, the young people of this *movimiente* were offering a plea for their families to be accepted into civic life. Where young Boomer protesters took to the streets, burning American flags to spite the adult world, Millennial protesters held flags high (including the stars and stripes) as they marched side-by-side with parents and older relatives.

Part Three

These youth-led demonstrations are an indication of what's to come from a generation that shows every sign of becoming a political powerhouse in the Twenty-First Century. As Millennials continue to enter young adulthood, they will bring this same civic engagement, institutional trust, and communal action to whatever they encounter in their communities, the nation, and the world.

What does the future hold for them? And what lies around the corner for the colleges, graduate schools, and employers that will confront a rising generation no longer in childhood? Millennials are not the only generation growing older—and, as a result, higher education faces some major transitions.

Over the next few years, Gen-X parents will take over from Boomers as the majority on college campuses. As parents of collegians, Gen Xers will differ from Boomers in broadly foreseeable ways. Even more fiercely protective than Boomers, they will apply to every facet of college life the same rigorous evaluation that they have applied to K-12 education, putting new emphasis on standards, data, transparency, real-time results, accountability, and cash value. As Gen-X entrepreneurs provide new market challenges, and as Gen-X corporate executives and public officials replace Boomers in top leadership roles, the world of higher education could experience profound shifts that may affect long-held institutional reputations.

Every year, more Millennials will graduate from colleges—and move on to graduate school, the workplace, and the ranks of alumni. This will have widespread implications for higher education.

In the coming era of greater accountability, career counseling services will rise in importance. Counselors will face increasing pressure to achieve specific results as Gen-X parents demand job placement and graduate earnings data to confirm the value of a high-cost education.

Graduate and professional schools will, in time, experience a turbulent new era, faced with increased scrutiny from Gen-X parents and public officials and new market challenges from Gen-X entrepreneurs. This could culminate in a major redefinition of institutional missions, a pressure to reduce costs, and fundamental changes in the markets for student applicants in certain fields.

Approached the right way, Millennial alumni could become even more active and engaged than those of prior generations—but with important new differences. Many more will be women. Development offices will have to think carefully about what they hope to get from them. Having paid far higher tuition bills than prior generations, and faced with far higher postgraduate debt, many will resist any notion that they should "give" to their alma maters any more than they already have.

As the collegians of today and tomorrow move into adulthood, the stakes will rise for them. So too will the stakes rise for America's colleges and universities. The Millennial influence on the world—and on colleges and universities—will continue long after they have left campus.

13 | From Boom to X: The Parent Transition

"Higher education must change from a
system primarily based on reputation
to one based on performance."

— REPORT OF THE COMMISSION ON THE FUTURE OF HIGHER EDUCATION
(U.S. DEPARTMENT OF EDUCATION, PRELIMINARY DRAFT, 2006)

From Boom to X: The Parent Transition

The arrival of Millennials on campus has been marked by helicopter parents—Boomer parents of Millennials who are sometimes helpful and sometimes annoying, but always hovering. Gone are the days of students and professors sequestered in ivy-covered buildings while parents attend to their own lives. Today's protective, ultra-attached parents make their presence and their agendas felt in every corner of college life.

The move toward increasing parental involvement at colleges began in the early 1990's when, for the first time, large numbers of Boomer parents began sending their Gen-X children to college. It gradually increased over the decade, as Boomers became the majority parents on campus. This rising parental involvement was then mostly seen as a good thing, an antidote to the sense of family (and community) detachment that had marked the 1980s. Parents were viewed as helpful partners in encouraging students to make good use of their college years, curb high-risk behaviors, and focus on career goals.

Once Millennials arrived at college starting in 2000, parental engagement, driven by new parental attitudes and the increasing closeness of family life, began to exceed what college officials felt was useful. By the time Millennials became the majority of traditional-aged college students in 2003, their increasingly active parents were perceived as intrusive, time-consuming, and annoying for college administrators and faculties. By the spring of 2004, when the first Millennials graduated, the term "helicopter parents" was in wide use.

The rise of helicopter parents came as a surprise to college officials. However, the trend was foreseeable to anyone who had been paying attention to trends among parents of preschoolers in the '80s, elementary students in the early '90s, and high schoolers in the late '90s.

Today another breaking wave is approaching: Gen-X "stealth-fighter" parents—even more protective, digitally keyed-in for constant surveillance, sharp eyes on the target, and ready to strike at a moment's notice to defend their children's interests.

Next year, Gen-X parents will become the majority of parents on campus tours. Between now and 2012, they will come to dominate the ranks of collegiate parents. In time, and they are likely to transform everything from the way classes are taught to the way college presidents think about the value of higher education.

Stealth-fighter parents will bring a range of new tactics to college parenting. When Boomer parents came to campus, a new light of public attention was cast on the collegiate experience. As Gen-X parents arrive, that light will become glaringly bright, more probing, less supportive—and, to some eyes, less welcome.

As the parental transition takes place, the world of higher education could experience institutional shifts unlike any seen in living memory.

The Changing of the Guard

At any time, people across a wide range of ages have key roles in campus life—from 17-year-old prospective students on up. Administrators and their staffs range in age from their twenties through their fifties. Faculty members tend to be a little older, trustees older still. Parents generally range from their forties to their sixties, but their ages tend to cluster more.

According to U.S. Census data, the median age of a mother at the birth of her college-bound child was 29 around 1990, and the median age of a father was 31 (these medians are about two years older than those for the entire population). To estimate the median age of a parent accompanying a high school senior on a campus tour, add 17 to 30, and you get 47—a little less for a mom, a little more for a dad. Subtract 47 from the calendar year, and you get the median birthyear of a parent on a campus visit. Subtract 50, and you get the median birthyear of parents whose children are actually attending college.

In 2007, the median birthyear of visiting parents is 1960—the final birthyear of Boomers. In 2008, the median birthyear will be 1961.

Hello, Mr. and Mrs. Generation X.

Starting in the spring of 2008, and for the next twenty-one years thereafter, Gen-X moms and dads will be a majority of those pouring over brochures, populating campus tours, checking out college rankings, worrying about costs, and influencing student choices about which school to attend. In the fall of 2008, the majority of freshmen will have Gen-X parents. Two or three years later, they will be the majority of parents paying tuition bills for undergraduates. Two or three years after that, they will comprise most of the proud moms and dads of graduating seniors.

Colleges may not feel the change right away, but sometime within the next ten years, probably early in the '10s decade, the transition from Boomer to Gen-X parents will reach a tipping point. The entire flavor of parent-college relationships will then take on a Gen-X quality that will be very different from what colleges now see with Boomer parents. From then on, Generation X will dominate the national discussion about higher education. Through the 2010s, colleges will be hugely aware of "stealth fighter" parents and the challenges they pose for colleges.

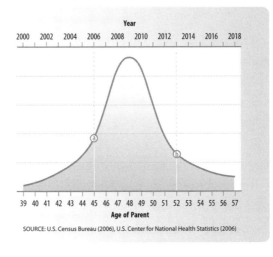

Distribution of All 18-Year-Old College Freshmen by Age of Eldest Gen-X Parents

Marked data points indicate when Xer parents represesnt:
(a) 19% of frosh
(b) 82% of frosh

SOURCE: U.S. Census Bureau (2006), U.S. Center for National Health Statistics (2006)

Major changes can and do occur in higher education whenever either a new student generation or a new parental generation arrives on campus. Generations tend to span about twenty birthyears. Approximately midway through each generation of college students, the generation of parents changes. This is because the first half of every generation is born mostly to parents of the second prior generation, and the second half is born mostly to parents of the immediately prior generation. Millennials born in the 1980s have mostly Boomer parents (born 1943–1960), while Millennials born in the '90s have mostly Gen-X parents (1961–1981).

Generational shifts have roughly coincided with specific decades over the past sixty years. Since World War II, some decades delivered a new generation of college students, others a new generation of college parents.

* 1950s — Silent students, G.I. parents.
* 1960s — Boomer students arrived.
* 1970s — Silent parents arrived.
* 1980s — Gen-X students arrived.
* 1990s — Boomer parents arrived.
* 2000s — Millennial students arrived.
* 2010s — Gen-X parents will arrive.

From one decade to the next, many of the changes in college life can be explained by these generational shifts.

To understand the generational shift that is coming, it is essential to recognize the real boundary between Boomers and Gen Xers. As we explained in *Generations* and *The Fourth Turning*, generational boundaries have real social and historical significance. These boundaries reflect each generation's shared "age location in history," from which its members draw a collective persona and a set of shared beliefs and behaviors that separates them from those born before and after.

Fertility patterns are only one factor to consider when defining the boundaries between generations. Viewed in socio-historical terms, Boomers were born between 1943 and 1960—not, as some demographers suggest, between 1946 and 1964. A Boomer fits a specific age location in history: too young to remember World War II, but old enough to remember when "Pleasantville" was still black and white. Recall George Lucas's *American Graffiti* ad: "Where were you in '62, before everything started to change?" The last-wave Boomers were just old enough to remember where they were in '62. Americans born in the early '60s do not often feel much kinship with them. Author Doug Coupland, himself born in 1961 (hence a "baby-boomer" according to some demographers) originally suggested the title "Generation X" for people born between 1961 and '64. Some of most prominent Americans who have set the tone for X—Michael Jordan, Quentin Tarantino, Jodie Foster, Barack Obama (who specifically defines himself as "post-boomer")—were born during these years.

As parents of collegians, Gen Xers will differ from Boomers in ways that are broadly foreseeable, given these generations' very different collective personas—and how differently they tend to recall their own educational experiences.

Boomers remember their experience with K-12 and higher education more positively, on the whole, than Gen Xers remember theirs. Even among Boomers who did not attend college themselves, there is a broad recognition that the college environment was a good thing for many of their peers, for their generation as a whole, and for the nation. Boomers have tended to want to replicate this positive generational experience for their own children (albeit with less risk-taking).

In contrast, far more Gen Xers remember their experience more guardedly, cynically, even negatively. Among Gen Xers who did not attend college, there is more of a mixed verdict about whether—given the time and cost—college was a good thing for people they knew and for their generation as a whole. Typically, they might say "yes" about some aspects of it, and "no" about others. As K-12 parents, Gen Xers have tended to want to protect their children from the academic deficiencies and family problems they recall from their own youth.

"Helicopters" in the Making

"I Am a Student! Do Not Fold, Spindle, or Mutilate!" read the signs of picketers outside Berkeley's Sproul Hall in 1964, mocking the computer-punch-card treatment the university was supposedly giving them. These vintage Boomers of the Free Speech Movement despised the life of duty and contentment, the supposed "intellectual and moral wasteland" of the world built by their parents. Earlier student protests had been the work of a lonely and polite few, but the Boomers at Berkeley swarmed and raged, resolving to "throw our bodies on the gears" to stop the G.I. Generation machine.

Within a few years, America's finest universities were awash in youth anger, as were its inner cities and military recruitment depots. In 1970, 44 percent of college students believed that violence was justified to bring about change. A clenched fist became the emblem, T-shirts and jeans the uniform, and corporate liberalism the enemy. College campuses had become the center of one of the most emotionally intense, culturally influential youth rebellions in American history.

Where Silent Generation "non-conformists" had feared blotches on their permanent records, Boomer collegians perceived few real risks in rebellion. Campus rioters broadly assumed that, the instant they deigned to do so, they could drop back into the American Dream Machine (after receiving "unconditional amnesty," often first on the long list of protester "demands"). Why not take a few years off to scream at the world, "find oneself," and pursue an inner calling? The same sort of comfortable life so easily mastered by their parents was always presumed to be within reach. For the most part, this sense of generational entitlement was vindicated as the first Boomer graduates poured into a rapidly expanding economy in the 1960s, when the rewards for a college education were soaring.

Many in this generation today recall their college years as the apotheosis of their lives, their years of collective catharsis, their linkage to the larger events of their time—much as the land and sea battles of World War II had been for so many of their parents.

As adults, Boomers came to associate some of the best and brightest of their generation with careers in education, ministry, and the media, in part because these professions were swiftly expanding to accommodate the large numbers of children born in the 1950s and early '60s. Boomers often still consider their peers at colleges and universities a key part of how their generation has made, and is continuing to make, its unique mark on the world.

Having gone to college when college was the place to be and when the rewards of an education seemed boundless, Boomer parents are inclined to think that college is nearly always worth the time and money for their children.

This positive memory has given many of them a powerful urge to participate in their children's experience with college. From filling out forms and touching up admissions essays to monitoring a daughter or son's every academic move and sipping brandy with the dean at graduation, they want to "be there"—for the good of their children and for their own enjoyment.

"Stealth Fighters" in the Making

From their '60s childhood through their '80s time on campus, Gen Xers learned young that they were largely on their own—and could not count on any institution, including schools, to watch out for their best interests.

When Gen Xers were in grade school, the Consciousness Revolution was in full boil. The divorce epidemic taught small children not to trust the most basic institution in their lives—the family. The film industry reflected the prevailing adult attitude with its strikingly negative portrayal of kids. In the 1970s, for the first time ever, U.S. economic data confirmed that children and teens had become the most poverty-prone age bracket. As women broke the glass ceiling and entered the labor market in vastly greater numbers before day-care was widely available, the era of the "latchkey child" had begun. In their quest to take care of their own needs, teens poured into the labor market and pushed youth employment to a post-war high. By the early '80s—with the surging popularity of business school and military careers, the rise of hip hop, and the emergence of a new style of brash young celebrities (Tom Cruise, Michael J. Fox, Eddie Murphy), the pop-culture image of youth began to shift toward a pragmatic, survivalist, market-savvy persona.

Through the Gen-X youth era, school reformers argued that kids would learn more if they were left more on their own and became "free agents" in charge of their own education. Teachers' pay declined dramatically, state initiatives and taxpayer revolts reduced the amount of (inflation-adjusted) public money available to schools, and in-school supervision was curtailed. The teaching of "the basics" was deemphasized as children were taught, in the words of Roland Barth, that "there is no minimum body of knowledge which it is essential for everyone to know." In 1983, as the first Gen Xers graduated from high school, the Department of Education declared a *Nation at Risk* from the "rising tide of mediocrity" emerging from America's public schools. From then on, one blue-ribbon commission after another told Gen Xers that their schools were failures, that they were stupid, and that they would never measure up against their far better educated global rivals.

In the early '80s, a new breed of college freshman arrived on campuses, focusing less on moral and cultural agendas and more on the bottom lines of higher education. Where a decade earlier, college kids were (in Charles Reich's term) "greening" their inner lives, students were now more intent on greening their wallets. Over 80 percent of college freshmen born before 1952 declared "developing a meaningful philosophy of life" to be a key goal of college, while just over 40 percent said the same about "being very well-off financially." By the mid-1980s, when Gen Xers filled campuses, these priorities had reversed: When asked the same question, only 40 percent were pursuing the philosophical goal, while nearly 80 percent were pursuing the financial goal. Their new question was: "Will it be on the exam?" If it wasn't, many wondered why anyone should care.

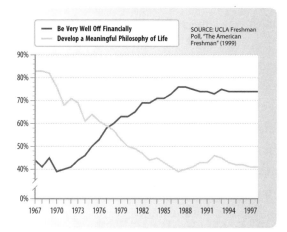

Figure 24 ▶

College Freshmen Survey, 1967–1998: Personal Objectives Considered Important...

The first Gen Xers entered college and the labor force just as the "Reagan Revolution" swept over America. In public policy, this meant deregulation, tax cuts, and skimpier safety nets. In the economy, it meant a new enthusiasm for markets, entrepreneurship, risk-taking, and individual empowerment. On the job, Gen Xers did not show the same penchant for self-discovery as Boomers. Instead, they sought out the highest-risk corners of the economy, exploring every cranny of the marketplace, seeking any entrepreneurial edge, taking one career gamble after another until one paid off big. For some, this worked out very well. For many others, it did not. Through the 1980s and '90s, the distribution of income and wealth spread substantially for all age brackets, but it spread the most for Generation X—leading to wry humor about how there was no longer any middle class left between the young temp workers and the young corporate lawyers, between the jaded "slackers" and the privileged "young fogies."

In the economy, the generation as a whole failed to show anywhere near the same income growth that prior generations did at the same age. In this new era, political leaders were free to disinvest in public education and infrastructure, business leaders to drive harder bargains with young workers, and union leaders to erect two-tier wage scales to protect older members. A rising tide of immigration and globalization drove down pay across many of the less-skilled sectors of the economy that have traditionally benefited the young. Since the late 1970s, adjusted for inflation, the annual earnings of full-time male workers aged 25 to 44 failed to grow at all. To get ahead, Gen Xers have had to work longer hours, take extra jobs, become dual income earners, go into business for themselves, or find novel ways to economize on their family's housing or schooling.

Given these realities, Gen-X attitudes toward their college experience were shaped by a pragmatism and survivalism that few Boomers ever felt. College elevated Boomers at a time when America looked to the youth culture for wisdom. College cast down Gen Xers at a time when America disparaged youth as ill-educated and undirected. Where Boomers had reveled in the whole college "experience," Gen Xers instead engaged in an energetic search for the right combination of courses, degrees, skills, and contacts that would give them a material edge. Where Boomers had wanted a way out of the "system," Gen Xers wanted a way into it.

For most Boomers, college was not a financial burden. Throughout the entire Gen-X college era—beginning in the early 1980s, when college tuitions first began to outpace inflation—the price of college weighed ever more heavily on families and forced students to incur ever larger student loans. Far more than Boomers, Gen Xers looked on college as a calculated market choice, with larger rewards (landing the right credential in a globalizing economy) but also with larger risks (coping with big debts on a small salary). In 2006, two books chronicled the plight of college graduates for whom the risks have outweighed the rewards—*Strapped: Why America's 20- and 30-Somethings Can't Get Ahead* (by Tamara Trout) and *Generation Debt: Why Now Is a Terrible Time to be Young* (by Anya Kamenetz).

Gen Xers have consequently developed a very different view from Boomers about their own generation's participation in, and relationship with, the field of education. With their pragmatic mindset, they tend to feel less at home with the heavily theoretical and ideological atmosphere of academe. Though Gen Xers believe strongly in lifelong learning, many also believe that the traditional college is only one of a multitude of settings in which people can educate themselves. As adults, they have gone on-line to wikis and encyclopedias, picked up courses at institutes and community centers, signed up for in-house corporate training, and become the first large generational market for distance learning programs. With a touch of irony, they have read "Dummies" and "Idiots' Guide" books on every imaginable subject.

They are determined not to let their own sons and daughters experience the same problems they recall from their childhood years. As PTA members, as voters, and—increasingly—as local, state, and national officials, Generation X has provided the most vocal constituency for school reforms that set standards, require transparency, impose accountability, and allow parents to remove their children from institutions that appear to be failing. They are the leading supporters of all forms of parental "choice" in education, from home schooling to vouchers to charter schools.

The Gen-X Factor

As Gen Xers replace Boomers in the ranks of collegiate parents over the next decade, the "no child left behind" parents of the K-12 world will become the "not with my child you don't" parents of higher education. Where Boomers have been interested in the public purpose of a college, in creating a more civic-minded society of educated people, Gen-X moms and dads tend to be more interested in its private purpose, in how higher education creates concrete opportunities for their own children.

To push their children toward a successful adult life, and to protect them from failure in college and beyond, Gen-X parents will exploit (and expect others to exploit) every available technology in the pursuit of every conceivable market opportunity. Applying the "FedEx" test to any college they meet, they will expect the service to be cheerful, fast, and efficient, providing information and options in real time, on-line, 24/7. Instead of arguing with administrators when their child encounters a problem, these parents will be likely to take quick and decisive action—filing a lawsuit, for example, or simply withdrawing a child from a school. Employers have already noticed this difference with Gen Xers as employees. When they don't like their boss, they don't talk, they walk. As collegiate parents, they'll walk with their child, if need be.

In K-12 schools, Gen-X parents have wanted standards—for schools, teachers, and students—data to measure the achievement of those standards, and transparency, giving them full and immediate access to all data. They have wanted accountability, for any schools and teachers that fail to achieve the promised results, along with bottom-line cash value, the confidence that, in the end, what was provided was worth all the investment of time and money. Above all, they have wanted as much choice as possible—for themselves, not their children. Gen-X parents will expect the same of colleges.

Whereas Boomer helicopter parents generally assume that the rewards of higher education are vast but impossible to measure, Gen-X stealth-fighter parents will be more likely to assume that anything immeasurable is untrustworthy—maybe just a feel-good con job. They will want proof that the money a student will spend and the debt a student will incur constitute a solid investment in that student's future. If one college charges a student $30,000 per year and another charges $20,000 per year, a Gen-X parent may ask what that extra $10,000 is actually buying. The following quip attributed to Education Secretary Margaret Spellings (herself a late-wave Boomer, born in 1957) speaks to many Gen-X parents: "In God we trust. All others bring data."

Parental opinions and priorities will become even more important in students' college choices. When Millennials co-purchase college with their Boomer parents, both are involved in the decision, but the parent is generally prepared to defer to the child's choice. Gen Xers will be even more involved and more directive. Under the rubric of parental protection, they will apply more of what one might call an "executive co-purchase," with the student more often asked to defer to the parent's choice of college.

In their children's college education, as with other expensive purchases, Gen Xers want a fair and open transaction, with complete and accurate information and unconstrained consumer choice. They will evaluate the transaction on the basis of the value it appears to offer. If they agree to it, they will expect results. If they fail to get results, they will demand consequences. As K-12 schools have already seen, these parents want administrators to run their schools like marketplace businesses—while they as parents have the freedom of marketplace consumers.

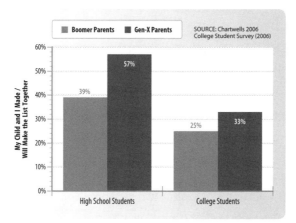

Figure 25 ▶

Boomer Parents versus Gen-X Parents: What role did/will you play in developing or selecting the list of colleges from which your child will choose?

Every cross-generational parent-child relationship triggers its own special challenges. Between Boomers and Millennials, the biggest source of friction has been the parental focus on values, authenticity, and inner-life goals. This has often clashed, in college and out, with the new youth interest in leading a conventional, achievement-oriented life. Between Gen Xers and Millennials, the source of friction will be somewhat different. Over their collective lifespan, Gen Xers have developed a pragmatic and individualistic—sometimes, even libertarian—approach to work, leisure, and education. This modular, market-oriented lifestyle will clash with the new youth interest in life balance and community building. As colleges now do with Boomers, they will have to balance the desires of the parents with those of their children.

Consumers in the College Marketplace

In their usual approach to the marketplace, Gen-X consumers are menu driven. They tend to compartmentalize, viewing every transaction as a series of discrete and categorical choices. A leading Gen-X entrepreneur, Michael Dell, has con-

Datatel 2006
College Parent Survey

The Datatel 2006 College Parent Survey, released by LifeCourse Associates and Crux Research, explores how today's college parents view their relationship with their children and with the colleges their children attend. From student achievement levels to college dining to student debt, the study confirms the new direction of Millennial collegians and the hands-on attitude of their parents. It also spotlights the breaking wave of Gen-X parents that will be hitting America's campuses in full force over the next ten years, bringing a new set of priorities to higher education. The following are a sampling of the results of these surveys.

The Hands-on Parent

Parents are continuing to stay protectively involved in the lives of their Millennial offspring even after they leave home. They report talking on the phone with their collegiate children an average of three to four times a week, and welcoming them home for visits seven or eight times each school year. Three quarters of the parents surveyed said that they were involved in their children's choice of academic major, and nearly 70 percent said they had some involvement in their children's specific course choices.

This has not always been the case with college students and their parents. Parents agree by four to one that they are more involved in helping their children succeed at college than their own parents' generation was, and, by two to one, they agree that they spend more time with their collegiate children then their parents spent with them at that age.

The particularly close Millennial-parent bond is fueling high expectations from parents for an active—even invasive—relationship with the colleges and universities their children attend. Parents said they would be extremely likely to intervene on behalf of their children when facing a variety of problems, from poor quality housing and food to unfair pay at a campus job to problems with class attendance and substance abuse. They overwhelmingly agree that colleges should allow them direct access to their children's grades, attendance records, health records, disciplinary records, and class schedules.

Parents realize that their collegiate children are more pressured and achievement conscious than prior generations were at that age, and they acknowledge their role in promoting these trends. They know that their children push themselves harder to do well in school than they did—perhaps because, as they also acknowledge, they push their children harder than their parents pushed them. Parents consider today's collegians to be more organized and more inclined to plan ahead than they themselves were at that age—and admit that that they pressure their children more in these areas than they themselves were pressured.

The Gen-X Factor

Even more than Boomer parents, Gen-X parents expressed an intense involvement in their children's lives and decisions. Half (49 percent) of all Gen Xers said that they began planning for their children's college education when the kids were in elementary school or younger, while only 38 percent of Boomer parents said the same. Gen-X parents played more active roles in developing the list of colleges from which their children would choose.

Gen-X parents communicate with their college-age children far more often than Boomer parents do. Gen-X parents are far more likely than Boomers to communicate with their collegiate children more than five times per week using email (27 percent to 17 percent), instant messenger (24 percent to 5 percent), phone (42 percent to 28 percent) and text messages (12 percent to 2 percent).

More Gen-X parents insist on greater transparency from their children's colleges. Both generations of parents agreed that colleges should allow them to see their children's grades, attendance records, health records, and other information. Two-thirds (67 percent) of Gen Xers said this was important, versus 48 percent of Boomers.

More than Boomer parents, Gen Xers rated the social and experiential component of a college education as very important—from the extracurricular activities to the alumni network to the chance to become a more "well rounded" person and join a student body with common values. Gen-X parents were four times more likely than Boomer parents to say that their children attended college in part to meet a potential spouse or life partner.

The data reflect disparities in how these two generation of parents view the financial burden of paying for college. Among parents of current collegians, Gen Xers expected their children to have higher levels of debt, and nearly twice as many expected that debt to affect their children's career choices. Gen Xers were more likely to rate the final cost of attendance and their children's probable debt levels as very or extremely important when evaluating colleges.

Gen-X parents have a greater focus on practical employment issues for their collegiate kids. More of them considered the earning capabilities of graduates when evaluating a college, and more cited "preparing for a specific career" and "earning a higher salary" as important reasons for their children to attend college. Virtually all (98 percent) of Gen Xers with children currently in college think schools should help students find jobs that relate to their major or their field, compared to only 79 percent of Boomers.

structed a global on-line computer hardware business in which consumers can pick and choose, buying exactly what they want, paying only what they must, and knowing exactly what they're getting, when they'll get it, and how. Not many Gen-X consumers want to buy a CD anymore when they can buy precisely the songs they want on iTunes and not pay for unnecessary extras.

Similarly, Gen-X parents are likely to wonder why they should purchase a whole college package that comes with a slew of expensive extras, which they may view as neither necessary nor useful to their particular child. Instead, they will tend to split the college experience into its components and pick and choose exactly what they want for their children. Every component will need to measure up. If any one does not, Gen-X parents will be inclined to go elsewhere for that piece of the product.

As consumers, these new college parents will be increasingly empowered by their peers, who will fill the ranks of administrators, business executives, entrepreneurs, and political leaders. As midlife Gen-X parents call for cost-effective college learning, midlife Gen-X entrepreneurs will find new ways to offer this learning outside of the traditional college setting—through for-profit institutes, in-house corporate training, distance learning, foreign colleges, and military service, among other possibilities. Gen Xers in public office may facilitate this trend by widening the standards for professional and academic certification.

To prepare for Gen X, college officials might reflect on precisely what constitutes the worth of the higher education "product" they offer. To do this, they might break down the college product the way Gen Xers implicitly will, in terms of its major components—*brand*, *experience*, and *learning*—and identify the cash value a school offers in each of these areas.

Brand is the reputation and name recognition associated with a college or university. Tuition purchases the chance to earn a diploma stamped with the college's brand, recognizable to the world and answering many questions that will be on the Gen-X parent's mind. What prestige will a college's graduate enjoy? What doors will the degree open? What edge will it give over a degree from elsewhere? What are a college's "honors" worth? How well will a college help a student get a job? A brand can sometimes focus on a specific region, gender, or ethnicity—or on a particular academic program or career path. It may be associated with an identifiable ideology, with private wealth or public service, with diversity, selectivity, or high endowments.

Experience is the non-academic life enrichment provided by a college, everything it offers outside of the classroom. What quality are the housing, food, outdoor spaces, athletic facilities, art studios, computer labs, lounges, and other amenities? What extracurricular activities are offered? What is the college's social scene like, from dating to the party culture to the general atmosphere of the campus and its surrounding locale? What other experiences are offered, such as internships, community service, study-abroad programs, and interaction with students from diverse backgrounds? Parents will perceive that the size and character of a college's student population will greatly affect the experience it can offer their child.

Learning is the academic component of a college, the knowledge taught in class. What specific knowledge is a student gaining? How well do the classes supplement material a student may have learned in high school? How well do the classes improve a student's writing and analytical skills? How will students' learning help after college—in postgraduate education, the workplace, and daily life? How does the curriculum address the needs of students who will graduate into the digital age? Does the college specialize in any particular fields? What size are the classes? How well equipped are they with modern technology? How interesting—and challenging—is the curriculum?

Gen-X parents will want to know what each of these three components—brand, experience, and learning—will be worth to their child. They may want to purchase one or two of them, but not the others that they deem unnecessary or unsatisfactory. Can a student take enough AP classes in high school to get a degree in less time, or transfer from a community college to get it for less money? Can a student attend a foreign college while paying tuition directly to that college, and get credit toward a degree at home? Can a student who spends most off-hours working at a job avoid paying student activity fees?

Implications for Recruiting and Admissions

The college brand is a major part of the college purchase, justifying much of its expense. Gen-X parents will tend to view the brand as something that will be associated with their child for a lifetime. Many a parent will be self-branding also, as the parent of a child who has earned admission to a particular college. This has been true with prior generations of parents, but with Gen-X parents it may become glaringly overt.

Stealth-fighter parents will be more inclined to demand proof of the college's brand strength—they will seek data supporting the quality and reputation of the school and how well it achieves its educational mission. Parents will also be inclined to look behind the usual national rankings. According to the Datatel 2006 College Parent Survey, some factors that now produce high rankings (faculty salaries, alumni giving, selectivity) are far less important to parents than data about student outcomes. More than Boomers, Gen-X parents will demand information—now seldom available—on the documented earning capabilities of graduates, the percentage who pursue careers in their fields of study, the percentage who drop out, and the size of loan repayment obligations. Gen-X parents may want to see data about outcomes for those who do not graduate, to evaluate the risks facing their own child.

Workplace readiness will factor highly into parental perceptions of a college's brand. Does a college have data about the career experiences of recent alumni? Does it have strong ties with local employers? If a small college in Chicago publicizes its internship program and its relationship with local business, it will stand out to parents who prefer that their children settle near Chicago.

The core element of a college's brand—the marketability of its diploma—will be more open to question than in recent decades. Gen-X consumers are well known for weak brand loyalties, what Douglas Coupland (who coined "Generation X") has referred to as "microallegiances." More than other generations, they take great effort to determine whether a branded product is really worth the price. In recent years, some liberal arts colleges have found that they could enhance their brand value in the eyes of Boomer parents (and raise the number of applications) simply by raising their tuition. This tactic will be much less successful with Gen-X parents, who will bring competition back to the pricing of luxury brands, including colleges. Boomers are famous for bragging about how much they've spent on a prestigious car or vacation.

College Rankings

Each year, college ranking guides influence thousands of students and parents as they sort through their many college choices. Millennials and their families want to know which schools are "the best," which work well for their specific needs and interests, and—with tuition and fees on the rise—which will be a worthwhile financial investment.

Perhaps the most famous of these guides is the *U.S. News and World Report's* "America's Best Colleges," first published in 1983, which evaluates colleges based on what it calls "widely accepted indicators of academic excellence." Data is gathered from each college for up to fifteen indicators, and each is assigned a weight reflecting its importance. The colleges in a given category (Research University, Liberal Arts College, and so on) are then ranked against their peers based on their composite weighted score.

Another popular rankings guide is the *Princeton Review's* "Best 361 Colleges." Using a very different model, *Princeton Review* creates sixty-two rankings lists based on survey responses from current students at each college. The lists cover a broad range of categories, including colleges with the most interesting professors, the most diverse student populations, the happiest students, the biggest sports scene, the most (or the fewest) parties, and even the best radio stations.

In recent years, many additional college ranking guides have flooded the market place. As these guides have grown in prominence, so too has a heated debate over their merits and drawbacks. The criticism of the guides is twofold.

First, critics contend that colleges find ways to rig the outcome by playing an elaborate numbers game with the indicators in the most popular guides (and the *U.S. News* rankings in particular). To boost their "yield," a college might accept more early decision students. To increase their average SAT score, they might give students with higher scores better financial aid packages. A college that plays this game shrewdly can move up several slots in a rankings guide without improving the educational experience of its students. Schools can also prioritize rankings indicators at the expense of other important factors. For example, a college that wants to raise its average SAT score may offer better financial aid packages to applicants with high scores, possibly decreasing the economic diversity of its student body.

Second, critics insist that the dominant college ranking guides do not truly measure

academic excellence, or anything else that would be useful to students and parents in making their college decisions. A number of alternative guides have sprung up in recent years, offering what they see as more insightful ways to rank the "best" colleges. The *Washington Monthly College Rankings*, launched in 2005, compares schools based on "what they are doing for the country" by advancing social mobility, economic growth, and an "ethic of service" among their students.

This second line of criticism raises a few key questions: What do Millennials and their parents really want to know about schools when choosing a college? How well do college rankings reflect the criteria that are most important to these consumers of higher education?

In 2006, LifeCourse Associates and Crux Research conducted two surveys that investigated these questions: the *Chartwells 2006 College Student Survey* and the *Datatel 2006 College Parent Survey*. We asked Millennial collegians and their parents what their priorities were in evaluating colleges—with a number of interesting results.

When Millennials and their parents were asked "how important would this be to you (and your child) when choosing a college," the responses of parents and students were in surprising agreement. The three factors most often rated by both as "very/extremely important" were:

- The final cost of attendance (most frequent response)
- How much debt the student is likely to have
- The graduation rate

Other factors parents and students considered top priorities included:

- The amount of time full-time faculty spend with students
- The earnings capabilities of graduates
- The percent of graduates who pursue careers in their fields of study
- The average score of a college on a national college learning evaluation for graduating seniors

Factors they considered less important included:

- The selectivity of a college
- The average high school class standing for the college's current students
- The percentage of the faculty that have Ph.D.s in their field
- The alumni giving rate
- How much the faculty is paid

College ranking guides do not reflect these priorities of Millennials and their parents.

None of the *U.S. News* indicators take into account parents' and students' top priorities of cost and debt-burden. Graduation rate is one of the indicators, but it is assigned a very low weight, only five percent of a college's rankings score—the same weight given to the alumni giving rate, which parents and students considered much less important. Meanwhile, many of the guide's top-weighted indicators rank relatively low on parents' and students' priority lists, including faculty salaries, the percentage of faculty with degrees in their field, student acceptance rate, and high school class standing.

In the years ahead, the consumers of college guides will include increasing numbers of Gen-X parents whose children are now reaching college age. This generation of parents is more likely to be wary of indicators that can be gamed by colleges and less likely to pay attention to rankings that do not reflect their priorities. They may even start turning away altogether from rankings that have been pre-digested and overtly gamed by colleges. More than Boomers, they will insist on unbundling the data so they can personally examine the numbers in exactly the areas in which they are interested. They may favor the approach used by the Princeton Review, which evaluates specific areas of academic and campus life and ranks colleges in each of them—leaving students and parents to determine which rankings matter most to them.

Gen Xers are more likely to brag about how little they've spent. Expect the same in college shopping.

To build and maintain their reputations, many colleges would do well to identify their brand niche—whatever differentiates them from others—and develop data to support their excellence in those areas. The goal is to make the "top three" list for the category in question. This need not coincide with *U.S. News* rankings or any other popular measure of excellence. Perhaps graduates from a community college have a surprisingly high acceptance rate into college nursing programs. Perhaps a college boasts the highest number of graduates employed with video game companies. Perhaps a college boasts the best first-year curriculum for any non-residential school within one hundred miles of Philadelphia. Perhaps a college has the best writing or engineering program in Texas. The key is to grab the attention of these menu-driven parents by being the strongest at *something* that they might want for their children.

Gen-X parents will bring to colleges the same focus on data-driven standards and accountability that they have applied to K-12 schools. Gen-X employers will pressure colleges to adopt explicit standards, and Gen-X legislators may require them. Colleges that become known for resisting this call for clearer standards and greater accountability may begin losing their ability to attract quality students. Similarly, colleges that rely on honors programs to attract top students may be called on to demonstrate in advance what standards those honors require.

The admissions process—with all of its various essays, tests, and other requirements—will come under increasing scrutiny. Whatever rules a college sets, stealth-fighter parents will become familiar with them, will expect them to be followed, and will demand that colleges keep documentation to defend the denial of admission or financial aid to any student. Gen-X parents will want to know if a school gives preference to celebrities, "legacies," or "development admits" (students from very wealthy families). This may attract some applicants and deter others, but will be more likely than before to crystallize into a public reputation that directly impacts the college's brand.

Implications for Campus Life

College students typically spend only about twelve hours per week in class. What students do with their other hours—from gathering in the library to catching the big soccer game, from attending parties to getting a little sleep—will define a major part of their college experience.

To satisfy Gen-X parents, a college has to provide quality services outside the classroom at a cost those parents will perceive as competitive. Housing and food are key. From the wiring of the dorms to the freshness of the vegetables, parents will not be satisfied with the same level of quality they recall from their own collegiate years. Bunk beds, shared bathrooms, and mystery meat will more often be seen as unacceptable, both by students and their parents.

At the same time, parents will expect to know the opt-in or opt-out price of every service a college provides so they can evaluate and compare its value. More parents than before will opt out of certain options if they do not consider them worth the money. More parents than before will want to purchase the highest-possible luxury in housing and food. Colleges need to strike a reasonable balance in responding to Gen-X parents who want to individualize their child's campus experience by price. While wanting to accommodate these parents, colleges do not want to be seen as violating the rising community ethic of Millennial students, many of whom will find their parents' opt-ins and opt-outs annoying and embarrassing.

Colleges need to be explicit about extracurricular offerings and support them with as much data as possible. Gen-X parents will be more likely than Boomers to think about how these activities will benefit their particular child, given his or her special needs and interests. The goal should be to serve the individual student—think "no collegian left behind"—rather than to entertain alumni or the campus community with grand events. For this, a school's extracurricular infrastructure needs to provide broad opportunities to the largest possible segment of the student body. Gen-X parents will be less impressed by a thousand-seat theater primarily used for visiting acts attended by older audiences, and more impressed by well-equipped black box performance spaces available to student troupes. They will not want to see a college's main athletic fields restricted to varsity teams only.

Gen-X parents will want students to have full access to extracurriculars during their freshman year—a year for which full tuition and fees are charged. Parents with a child who was the editor of a high school paper may not tolerate a two- or three-year wait before the student can join a college paper staff.

Gen-X parents will look to secure a quality social experience for their collegiate children. According to Datatel 2006 College Parent Survey, they are more openly protective than Boomers. Many will want to shelter their children from certain behaviors—partying, substance abuse, or whatever else a parent may find objectionable. More will insist upon housing options that reflect those preferences—substance-free dorms, single-sex dorms, honors dorms, ethnic dorms—whether or not their children want this (which many will not). The Datatel survey also confirms that Gen-X parents, pragmatic as always, are much more likely than Boomer parents to say that their children chose a college "in part to meet a potential spouse or life partner."

Stealth-fighter parents will want data on these activities. On-line resources such as Security on Campus, Inc., and the National Survey of Student Engagement will multiply and become more user-friendly and accurate. Colleges can earn kudos from parents by collecting and publicizing these statistics on their own—not just about the usual demographic factors (geography, male-female ratios, ethnic diversity), but also about crime, accidents, substance abuse, and the hours per week students spend studying, socializing, or attending school events. Rather than leaving it to the *Princeton Review* to rank a college high or low among "party schools" or in other areas of campus life, schools can develop their own data to present the college experience to Gen-X parents in a way that more accurately conveys their educational missions.

Gen-X parents of special-needs children will be even more vigilant than Boomer helicopter parents have been—truly earning those stealth-fighter wings. Many will expect to remain (and expect back-home physicians and other advisors to remain) just as involved in their child's "support team" as they were in high school. Whatever counseling or other support services a school promises, it had better deliver.

When dealing with Gen-X parents whose protective instincts have been roused, colleges must have firm boundaries of conduct. Even more than with

Boomers, colleges need to institute a very explicit "division of labor" that encourages parents to participate in certain areas of college life while asking them to back off and allow the college full jurisdiction over others. At orientation, colleges can provide actual lists of the primary do's and don'ts. Colleges may also wish not just to allow, but to encourage FERPA waivers, especially for special-needs students. If any student has unexpected health problems with bad results, stealth-fighter parents—and their lawyers—will not be calmed by any suggestion that the student's privacy rights had to be respected.

Colleges must always keep in mind that Gen Xers perceive them as one among many providers in a large marketplace. New competitors will emerge, providing alternative choices for much of what colleges provide. This is already common with housing and food services, but could soon extend to counseling, extracurricular activities, internships, foreign study, and other social and cultural experiences. Colleges might want to keep an eye on the competition as it emerges. If that competition offers better quality for less money, many Gen-X parents will steer their children in that direction.

Implications for the Classroom

Gen-X parents will tend to view their children as lifelong knowledge consumers, the same way they view themselves. However, these parents will not want to see their children reaching back later in life to learn the basics, as so many Gen Xers are still doing. After investing a great deal of money in their children's education, they will not want to see them buying books with the words "dummy" or "idiot" in the title.

Many of these parents will view course work in stark cash-value terms. Tuition at an elite private college or university today is about $4,000 per semester course, which covers about 40 hours of classroom time. Each hour of class therefore costs roughly $100. That's about the same cost per hour as prime seating at a Paul McCartney concert, and three times the cost per hour of attending an NFL game or Broadway show. When paying for college classes, students and parents are investing in a very expensive stack of tickets. Apart from the degree that students may eventually earn and whatever they are doing outside of class, parents will ask: Precisely what are we buying? What earnings potential is my child gaining from this class?

Gen-X parents will expect class time to be well spent. They will want to know who is actually teaching—is it the full professor listed in the course guide or an inexperienced teaching assistant—and whether a teacher is actually showing up for all classes and is always available during office hours. Then they will ask about the quality of teaching: Is it interesting and engaging? Is it nothing but scripted lectures? Ever mindful of markets and technology, many Gen-X parents will wonder why a college pays a full faculty salary to a teacher whom students find uninteresting when it could digitally pipe in presentations from a world-famous professor and then organize the teaching assistants to handle discussions, questions, and exams. They will want to know: Is anyone at this college even considering such innovations?

Gen Xers will be far less willing than Boomers to sit quietly as their collegiate children are asked to prepare ponderous term papers and hand-write final exams—skills many parents will perceive as no longer useful. If digital multimedia technologies are not part of the classroom experience, they will want to know why. If the entire class time is devoted to a student taking notes from a lecture, they will ask why that information could not have been posted on a web site, or put into the students' pockets via "course casting," with classroom time used more effectively for questions and discussion. They will expect reading, writing, editing, and research skills to be taught more in line with what they perceive that today's workplace will require.

Gen Xers' expectations about college curricula will reflect their own view of the world. They will expect science to be current and math to have direct application. They will want greater attention paid to the histories, cultures, and languages of the Middle East, East Asia, and Latin America—and less to Europe. They will expect social sciences to be taught objectively, without being overwhelmed by a professor's political point of view. They will prefer liberal arts curricula to focus on the classics, on baseline knowledge that every educated person should grasp. In their eyes, a college that teaches an ideological, dull, or outdated curriculum will do nothing to increase the earning potential of its graduates—and that makes tuition a bad investment.

Writing in the Digital Age

Millennials have no memory of what writing was like before the digital age. While earlier generations have had to adjust to other technologies, Millennials are the first post-stone-age generation for whom writing has never centered on a pen or pencil and some sort of paper.

From text messages to email to instant messenger, typing has crowded out other forms of communication—both written and oral—for today's young people. Occasions for writing by hand are particularly scarce. This generation has been keyboarding and printing assignments throughout their education. Increasing numbers are bringing laptops to class, eliminating the need for hand-written notes.

Meanwhile, schools are spending less and less time teaching Millennials the skills of writing by hand. In the 1940s and '50s, most teachers insisted on as much as two hours a week of handwriting instruction. Until the 1970s, penmanship was a separate lesson each day through the sixth grade—and usually was graded. According to a Vanderbilt University survey, today's primary grade teachers tend to spend ten minutes a day or less on penmanship, while many schools now teach computer and keyboarding skills as early as kindergarten.

Despite the fact that students no longer have much experience or practice in writing by hand, older educators continue to expect Millennials to excel at this traditional skill during the most critical moments of their academic life—when taking exams. In most colleges, and many high schools, the "blue book" essay exam is still the norm. The "free response" sections of the Advance Placement tests are to be answered in longhand, as is the new handwritten essay section of the revamped SAT, introduced in 2006. In its first year, only 15 of the nearly 1.5 million students who took the SAT wrote their essays in cursive. The rest scrawled their answers as best they could in block letters.

The challenge most Millennials face during a handwritten exam goes deeper than just the act of handwriting itself. In transforming the physical act of writing, computers have also transformed the way students *think* as they write. Older generations of students learned to construct a linear narrative in their mind before recording it through pen or typewriter. Today, students learn to form their ideas in any order, adding to their thoughts and sometimes re-organizing as they write—and cannot remember a time when writing was done any other way.

If a college wants to evaluate students by means of an essay exam, it should allow the students access to the same digital technology that they use to express themselves whenever they are *not* taking an exam—and that they will later use in the workplace, in professions, and perhaps as professors themselves. More broadly, colleges need to re-think how well they are integrating technology into their curricula. Are students asked to jump through traditional hoops just because today's older generations once had to do the same? Or because those hoops are convenient for some professors who are uncomfortable with newer technologies? Alternatively, are students given cutting-edge tools to train for their fields in the same way they would someday be expected to perform?

While Boomer parents and professors (along with older generations) consider a tenured faculty to be a permanent fixture of the academic chain of being, Gen-X parents will be more willing to question why they are not subject to the same bottom-line incentives and market forces that most Gen Xers face daily in their own jobs. They will raise new questions about how much tenured faculty are paid, how much they actually teach, what personal access students may have to them, and whether their classes and teaching styles are relevant to today's workplace.

If Gen-X parents are displeased with classroom learning in traditional college settings, Gen-X entrepreneurs will provide them with other options. Many

The Revolution in Educational Technology

Millennials are coming of age at a time of unprecedented techno-logical change, which colleges are harnessing to enhance their students' learning experiences. These new educational tools range from instructional software to educational management systems (such as Blackboard), from high definition flat-panel multimedia to in-class clickers that allow students to "vote" on snap quizzes, from on-line libraries and databases to sophisticated design-and-analysis tools (such as CAD) for budding scientists and engineers.

Millennials will gravitate toward—even insist upon—information technologies that simplify and streamline their educational needs. Fancy gadgets alone won't impress; they have to work sensibly in real-world settings.

Because Millennials like to work in teams, colleges can pay special attention to technologies that allow students to collaborate on group projects and to create different kinds of "virtual communities" for the purpose of research, experimentation, model building, essay review, and final evaluation. This is how large institutions can replicate some of the advantages of a small college. Because Millennials also value contact with the best thinkers, lecturers, and data banks in any field, colleges can establish high bandwidth access to other universities and to research institutes and government agencies the world over. This is how small institutions can duplicate some of the advantages of a large university.

Many institutions of higher learning are harnessing on-line digital technology to construct a whole new model of education known as "distance learning." According to Eduventures, a leading education market research firm, approximately 1.2 million students were taking on-line higher education programs at the close of 2005, a number that, by all accounts, is still climbing. Accreditation of distance learning programs has become a source of continuing policy debate. Many new programs seek to join the ranks of already-accredited schools that have long specialized in on-line education (like the University of Phoenix), while many traditional colleges still question the legitimacy of any program that does not center around face-to-face learning.

Over the last few of years, a growing number of traditional colleges have been changing their minds. The potential revenues are too large to pass up. According to International Data Corporation, the number of colleges offering some sort of distance learning program rose from 62 percent in 1998 to 87 percent in 2004. In 2007, the Massachusetts Institute of Technology will complete its pioneering "OpenCourseWare" project, making all MIT course material available to anyone in the world on the Internet, free of charge—a powerful example that will help legitimize the Internet as a platform for higher education. Other colleges are following suit, from Yale to Notre Dame to Bryn Mawr, making lecture notes, sample tests, or even video files of lectures publicly available on the Internet.

After this rapid recent growth, the future for distance learning remains uncertain. On the whole, most Millennial collegians yearn for a flesh-and-blood rite of passage, an education that isn't just about knowledge and skills, a community of peers who work and play and live together. But there are two subgroups who might continue to fuel rapid growth in distance education for colleges that target them effectively. First, many high-aptitude male teens may prefer to take distance learning classes rather than taking part in a campus life, either because they dislike school or because they are currently in the military service or otherwise employed. For these individuals, a college might introduce a distance learning option as part of a larger personal plan, through which they might apply later on to become an on-campus student. Second, there are millions of affluent students abroad who would like an American education but may not have the means—or, in an era of tightening visa policies, the opportunity—to attend.

Over the next few years, the explosion of distance education will receive a boost from the growing numbers of Gen-X entrepreneurs (on the supply side) and Gen-X college parents (on the demand side). Gen Xers are more market oriented, more technologically savvy, and less attached to traditional educational models than their Boomer counterparts. College officials should carefully monitor this trend. A competitive market will eventually produce competitive pricing, and the increasing supply of distance learning programs could well result in dramatic downward price push for all forms of higher education Alternative options in the higher education market will put increasing pressure on colleges to justify the value of their more traditional (and often higher-cost) campus-based programs.

market alternatives for traditional post-secondary education already exist—most notably, distance learning—as the digital age continues to reduce the cost of quality instruction. What it lacks in face-to-face interaction, distance learning can make up in 24/7 convenience. For a college to compete, it must offer a personal and exciting experience with high-quality faculty and cutting-edge technology—and offer it to every student, starting freshman year, not just to a handful of seniors in seminars. If a college fails to do so, stealth-fighter parents will take their business—and their college-age children—elsewhere.

Thus will Gen-X parents bring the principles *No Child Left Behind*—and the K-12 standards movement—to higher education.

14 | Graduation and Beyond

"The young men and women of America's future elite work their laptops to the bone, rarely question authority, and happily accept their positions at the top of the heap as part of the natural order of life."

— DAVID BROOKS (2001)

Graduation and Beyond

As Millennials graduate and become alumni, the stakes will be high—not only for the graduates themselves, but for the colleges they leave behind.

For today's young people, that first job or that acceptance into graduate school will be the culmination of twenty years of education and planning. They (and their parents) will want all the years of studying, test-taking, and résumé-building to end in success. As these young graduates enter the job market with a new set of working styles, preferences, and skills, employers will start using different recruiting techniques—and reorganizing working environments—to attract and retain them. Some employers will get this new generation right on their own, while others will look to campus career-services officials for help.

As institutional reputations fluctuate in the coming decades under pressure from Gen-X parents, Millennial alumni, with their institutional loyalty and belief in big brands, will cement new reputations in place. Colleges that can show that they equip their Millennial graduates for successful futures, and maintain good relationships with them as young professionals, will be in the best position to benefit from this re-branding.

Implications for Career-services

Already, today's college career counselors feel more pressure to achieve results than ever before—a pressure that will increase with the advent of Gen-X parents, causing career counseling services to rise in importance among collegiate functions. Counselors will be urged to produce data on job placement and graduate earnings to confirm the value of a high-cost education. They will notice more people looking over their shoulders in search of the bottom line, from protective parents to the student's "team" (hired consultants, lawyers, physicians, psychiatrists) and the media.

Most career counselors understand that the placement services they provide are affected by cyclical ups and downs in the economy. Unlike admissions officials, who can count on a predictable number of admissions slots, career counselors cannot count on a steady flow of job opportunities. This unpredict-ability will provoke more anxiety among today's collegians than it did for Gen Xers or Boomers at that age. Millennials, on the whole, have led more struc-tured lives through K-12 and college than prior generations did. They like to plan ahead, and they assume that other people are watching out for them to make sure everything goes well. The end of formal education and the need to confront the vagaries of the job market are coming as a shock to many of today's graduates. The high price of education and the burden of college loans adds to the anxiety many feel about this plunge into the "real world." Student debt is also changing the choices young people make as they enter the job market. According to the 2006 Chartwells College Student Survey, over 50 percent of Millennial collegians say that their college debt levels will in some way affect their career choices.

The college class of 2006 has so far been lucky in this plunge. They have benefited from a relatively favorable job market, a trend that could continue. However, the job market this year or next is not the foremost issue on the minds of Millennials. These graduates do not just want to land whatever job may be available. Instead, they want the "right first job" in a well-chosen career that will lead to a productive and successful life over a number of decades. Afterwards, they want to feel secure in their career choices through any future upturns and downturns in the national economy.

While career-services officials cannot be omniscient about the future, they can pay close attention to structural labor market trends. They can also encour-age students to do the same, while helping them identify local, national, and global sectors that are either expanding now or can be expected to grow in future decades. Some fields will be more accessible to Millennials than they were to Boomer or Gen-X collegians. Others will not. This is the case for every generation of graduates, but is particularly important to Millennials because of their desire and tendency to plan ahead.

The following occupational areas will experience predictable retirement waves over the next decade can provide distinct opportunities to this rising generation. Some examples:

* **Primary and secondary school teaching.** From the mid 1960s to the early '70s, a growing number of early-wave Boomers were hired to teach the very large cohorts then entering the school system. Now, four decades later, this critical mass of teachers is retiring, leaving openings for young hires.

* **Civil service.** All levels of government (federal, state, and local) experienced enormous employment growth from 1965 through 1980. Given early civil service retirement, the Silent Generation has by now almost entirely departed while Generation X was never hired in large numbers. This leaves a monogenerational (Boomer) civil service now rapidly approaching retirement.

* **Large manufacturing and natural resource corporations.** Many large corporations in traditional sectors like autos, steel, chemicals, and fossil fuel and mineral extraction have aging workforces. Large productivity gains allowed them to cut costs by "rightsizing" and "downsizing" in recent decades, leading to work forces heavy on Boomers and light on Gen Xers. A great number of entry-level Millennials will soon be required, not only in blue-collar jobs, but also at all professional and managerial levels.

Demographic and societal trends also point to major growth in health care, defense, homeland security, and personal services. Global trends suggest growth in energy, technology, and environmental sciences. Most of these high-growth employment opportunities constitute a reasonably good fit to the collective Millennial personality. Large durable organizations can offer the sort of career planning, collaboration, and large-scale projects that many Millennials seek. Government agencies now dominate the list of "ideal employers" cited by today's new college grads, according to Universum Communications, reflecting this generation's desire to build a stronger national community.

As Millennials graduate, so will increasing numbers of well-educated young people around the world. As Thomas Friedman has observed in *The World Is Flat*—and as career counselors and students are quite aware—many jobs can be outsourced at lower costs to college-trained youths in other countries. The pressure to compete globally will be a new reality in the professional lives of today's graduates. The bottom line will be intense salary competition, which could eventually climb the human resource "value chain" and affect such fields as accounting, marketing, finance, and law, much as global work force competition has already affected product and design specialties (such an engineering and software) in recent years.

The task facing students—and career service officials—is to identify and pursue those paths where American college graduates will have a substantial and enduring advantage over those from other countries. Three basic strategies are available to Millennials.

The first strategy is for students to choose careers that lean heavily on ties to a local community or local customers, first-class language or writing skills, or intimate familiarity with American culture and lifestyles.

The second strategy is to specialize in fields that leverage invention and creativity, which on the whole are nurtured better in the U.S. than in other countries. In today's global economy, the "left brained" (creative) skills are harder to outsource than the "right brained" (technical) skills. Students who wish to enhance their competitive edge can combine a liberal arts background—including, perhaps, some aspect of the creative arts—with the engineering, science, digital technology, or other degree required for their chosen fields. They may also want to steer their careers toward organizations in which older Boomer or Gen-X "creatives" are creating a durable global brand.

The third strategy is for students to move toward careers and organizations that leverage collaborative teamwork, playing to a natural Millennial strength. The whole "free agent" premise of globalized outsourcing is that the value of each worker is the same regardless of how that worker's job might be shifted between companies or countries. The premise of collaboration, on the other hand, is that the right organization can vastly enhance the economic value that workers might otherwise have individually. Using team-oriented information technology and empowered by "collaborative innovation" (or "swarm") networks, Millennials can build the kind of positive-sum organizations that may provide bulwarks against global outsourcing. As future voters, Millennials may try to push this trend by favoring legislation that encourages longer-term job tenure and closer workplace cooperation.

For Millennials, post-graduate employment will depend as much on local as on national or global conditions, because of the increasing closeness of family ties and the widening cost-of-living differentials between different regions—a factor of particular importance for debt-impacted students. States that have been losing youth populations may find themselves better positioned than before to keep well-educated young people who are not affluent from moving away. Today it is not as easy for Millennials as it was for young Gen Xers or young Boomers to leave small towns and cities and go look for a job in New York or Los Angeles. Moreover, today's collegians are less inclined to tolerate the high-stress lifestyle that many of today's highest-paying fields would require through their twenties. Many will prefer a good work-life balance in places with affordable housing. In time, Millennials may give these previously "uncool" regions a youthful new image and modern cachet—while recasting today's expensive cities and their exurbs as graying bastions for older generations.

With regional considerations becoming more important, colleges can develop useful relationships with local employers. This can include active efforts to generate nearby job opportunities for every new graduating class. It can also include close consultation with employers about specifications for job readiness and efforts to revise curricula to meet local economic needs. This can be done by colleges individually or through consortia—locally, regionally, or (through national associations) on a national or even international level.

Today's young adult workers prefer employers that offer teamwork, fairness, fewer job definitions, protection against risk, solid work-life balance, and longer career plans—while allowing closeness to parents. Millennials are also less entrepreneurial, less risk-taking, and more likely to consider long-term benefits than Gen Xers were as young workers and job seekers. In a recent Universum survey, collegiate job seekers rated 401(k) retirement plans and life insurance as more important factors than stock options or increased vacation time. They also rated a "good benefits package (stability)" as more important than a high starting salary.

Career counselors can tap into these aspirations by developing a career-services curriculum that adds structure to the task of settling on a career and finding the best possible first job. Millennials are more inclined to want—and need—this kind of structure than Gen Xers at that age. The less a student's prior workplace experience, the more that student will need such structure—and the more a student's parents will want it in a college. Neither Millennial students nor Gen-X parents will accept the idea of paying tuition (or amassing debt) for an education whose terminus is work irrelevant to a field of study, or—worse—unemployment.

A Four-year "Career-services Curriculum"

In this dawning era of "No Collegian Left Behind," career-services officials will find it useful to think of themselves—and present themselves—as comparable to an academic department. The four years of college, and the summers in between, can be described to students as a structured learning experience leading to career launch.

During the freshman year, incoming students can be made to feel as high priority as older students in the career counseling center. They could receive a mandatory career-services orientation (open to parents), at which they meet the career-services staff and learn about the college's four-year pre-employment plan. Counselors can encourage first-year students to take exploratory courses that may help identify career options—including courses or extracurricular activities that can enhance creativity in a wide range of fields. Right at the start, counselors can alert students about the need to safeguard their on-line reputations (and not use their names with anything they would not want a future prospective employer to find). Career-services staff can provide short seminars on the summer job search, especially for the rising number of students who arrive at college without ever having held a paying job. The post-freshman summer is an excellent time for students to learn what kinds of work they enjoy, what they can do well, and what they might usefully learn in their remaining three years in college. Students who are struggling financially will need to combine these career-defining goals with earned income to help cover their college costs.

For the sophomore year, career-services counselors can offer special courses teaching basic workplace economics, covering how salaries are determined in today's globalized marketplace, basic workplace skills, how to locate a job, how to get hired for a job, and what to do on the job. These courses can address the criticisms one often hears from today's employers—that today's new hires expect too much praise and feedback and have trouble dealing with setbacks and accepting criticism. The recent Partnership for Twenty-First Century Skills survey found a deep reservoir of complaints about "soft skills" (attendance, punctuality, attire), weak business communication skills, and a lack of assertiveness. Students who have never held a job should be encouraged to get one during this sophomore year—or, at the latest, during the following summer.

If pre-workplace courses are made mandatory, perhaps for credit, during the fall of the sophomore year, no students will slip through the cracks. Parents—and local employers—will appreciate knowing that no collegian will miss out on basic workplace orientation. If such courses are left optional, a number of students can be expected not to take advantage of them. At a minimum, parents can be advised of these programs and asked to urge their children to make full use of them.

Career counselors can teach basic job interview and deportment skills, from handshakes and looking people in the eye to knowing what to wear and speaking without word weeds and stumbles. A growing number of colleges have started to offer "etiquette courses," including everything from business vocabulary to mock formal dinners. By the end of sophomore year, all students should have basic workplace skills.

During the junior year, students at most colleges are required to commit to an academic field of concentration. This, they should be clearly told, will shape their qualifications for various career and job options. The junior year is a good time for career-services counselors to urge students to make a preliminary decision about one or two career paths. Counselors can go more in-depth with students about the skills of job-researching—a very different task now than just five years ago. They can teach students about employment search engines, on-line background information on prospective employers, résumé placement sites, and other new digital-age options. They can also teach skills of cover letter writing, résumé preparation, and email etiquette.

Summer employment after the junior year comes with higher stakes. Counselors can encourage students to engage in carefully focused research for possible jobs and internships. For some, this can be an opportunity to persuade an employer to offer a full-time position after graduation. Even jobs that will not lead to post-graduate employment can give students valuable credentials and experience in their chosen fields.

During the senior year, the collegiate job search will reach its familiar moment of seriousness, nothing new for 21-year-olds over the past several generations. For Millennials, though, this may be accompanied by greater personal anxiety, reflecting a new youth perception about the enormous significance of the "first real job." Today's collegians (and their parents) often consider their first job as a strategic career launcher, the payoff for all the planning, stress, and shared ambition that will have gone into the students' lives. This terrific first-job pressure is leading a growing number of graduates to opt to live at home and remain unemployed, and perhaps even to take temporary unskilled jobs, rather than make the wrong first career move.

With their lifelong optimism, Millennial graduates often have unreal expectations of what that first job will in fact be like. With so much weighing on their success, these young graduates are likely to feel derailed, even permanently damaged, when things don't go as planned—whether a bad relationship with a boss, difficulty getting along with coworkers, disappointment over work they may be asked to do, or (especially) getting laid off or fired. During the job search, counselors can offer practical lessons in how to avoid the most common problems in entry-level jobs. They can teach strategies for coping with disappointment, maintaining perspective when things do not work out as intended, and laying plans for what to do next. After students graduate, counselors can remain part of "the team" in the same way so many secondary school teachers and counselors have remained so important in the lives of Millennial collegians. In particular, counselors can stay in touch with recent graduates who have yet to find that "first job," offering to provide ongoing advice and assistance through emails and phone calls.

If a college gives a high priority to career counseling—developing a clear and effective career-skills and job-search curriculum, providing hands-on help with summer and graduate employment, and maintaining availability for postgraduate assistance—that college can powerfully enhance its brand in the eyes of prospective students and their parents. This branding can be reinforced by a college's commitment not just to make these services available, but also to make sure all students avail themselves of these services—including students who might be reluctant to use them. Such a college would thereby announce to prospective students and their parents that it takes very seriously the personal aspirations of its students and the practical applications of the education they receive.

Implications for Graduate and Professional Schools

Vis-à-vis this rising generation, graduate schools are right about where colleges were in the year 2002. The first Millennials (born in 1982) are now in their third year of graduate school, and the media glare is just starting to follow them. No national commissions have been convened, no heated public discussions launched, no major entrepreneurial challenges have arisen, and no probing questions have come from parents—not yet.

When these questions arise, they will focus first and foremost on cost. Over the past two generations, tuitions at graduate and professional schools have risen at least as fast—in some cases faster—as tuitions at undergraduate institutions. At Ivy League schools, post-graduate tuitions are now more than three times higher than they were in 1970, after adjusting for inflation. At state universities, postgraduate programs that once were nearly or totally free now come with substantial costs. Where colleges commonly offer grants to low-income or high-achieving students, graduate and professional schools do so far less often. Nearly all physicians and lawyers in their mid-sixties and older (born before 1943) left graduate school with no debts whatsoever. Today, debts in the range of $150,000 are common, and some students finish business, law, or medical school with debts of well over $200,000. To date, the impact of these very large debts has fallen on Gen-X students. As Millennials replace them—and as Gen Xers begin to view student debt from parental and legislative perspectives— the magnitude and impact of these debts will become more controversial.

Graduate and professional schools will start feeling the influence of Gen-X parents around 2013, the year the first Gen Xers turn 52, the median age for parents of college seniors. Around that time, large numbers of Gen-X legislators will be replacing Boomers in state houses and the U.S. Congress, bringing a new emphasis on standards and accountability to higher education. Also around then, Gen-X entrepreneurs are likely to be launching new market-driven challenges in higher education, including less costly routes to professional licenses and credentials. Faced with this four-pronged assault—media, parents, legislators, and entrepreneurs—post-graduate education will encounter a sharp new scrutiny.

Gen-X parents will compartmentalize post-graduate education as they did undergraduate education, separating it into the "brand," "experience," and "learning" components—but they will put less emphasis on the experience component and focus more on the market power of the brand and the cash-value of the learning.

Every field of post-graduate education will face some very basic questions: Why is each step of schooling necessary for competence in a field? Why must it take so long—and cost so much? Why should high-tuition programs provide the only entry into certain professions? Within each field, every school can be prepared to answer another set of questions. What jobs do recent graduates get? How much do they earn? How long does it take to pay off their debts? What's the graduation rate? What happens to dropouts—and how large are their debts? Gen-X parents and Gen X-led legislatures will press graduate schools to justify exactly what they are offering for the price they charge and the length of time their degrees require—and may demand sweeping measures to reduce costs and risks for students.

The pressure to justify costs and provide accountability may be particularly significant for law schools in the face of competitive pressure on the salaries of young lawyers, high levels of workplace attrition, cloudy prospects for traditional partnerships, and the growing number of students who want the degree for nontraditional reasons. Where prior generations of law students broadly assumed that a legal education would pay for itself in time, Millennials and their parents will start carefully evaluating the benefits and the risks. What happens to graduates who find a government or small-firm job paying $50,000 annually (the recent median, in some states), of which a full quarter must go to debt service? What happens to the graduates who cannot find any job? What about the 36 percent of all graduates who initially fail the bar exam? What about students who discover they do not want to be lawyers after the first year and leave law school with $50,000 in debt and nothing to show for it? The necessity of the third year in law school may also come into question, as students and parents consider whether the added learning justifies the cost and the time.

Ph.D. programs often provide free tuition and supplementary stipends in return for teaching or research duties, enabling many graduates to finish school with fewer debts. Even so, universities will face more probing questions about what their Ph.D. (and post-doc) students are accomplishing from one year to the next. Many Ph.D. programs require a minimum of four years to complete, but often that stretches to six or seven years. More Millennials, parents, and perhaps even legislatures will start asking why. In time, universities may be pressed to establish formal time tables and deadlines for graduate education, with some clear connection to what is necessary to achieve expertise in a field. Through the 2010s, the requirements for a number of fields that employ Ph.D.s could substantially change. If, in the Gen-X parent era, college faculties are expected to be more classroom-oriented and less research-driven, the credentials required for university teaching may be revised.

High-tuition graduate and professional programs that train students for modestly paying careers may have to accept the fact that increasing numbers of their graduates will use these degrees to enter other, higher-paying professions. Schools in fields such as public policy, public health, education, and ministry—many of which grew rapidly in the '70s when tuition was much lower—can expect a larger proportion of their graduates to seek high-paying jobs that serve private rather than public interests. If a school wishes, it can re-brand itself to accommodate this trend by altering its faculty, recasting its curricula, and adjusting its marketing. However, schools that try to maintain their original Boomer-era goals and ideals while charging Millennial-era tuitions may be perceived as not worth the money, regardless of their reputations.

After seventeen straight years of competing for grades, Millennials are even more likely to feel utterly stressed out on graduation day than Boomers and Gen Xers did in their own time. But how they react to this stress may be unfamiliar to older generations. Some freshly minted Millennial grads, after only a few weeks time, will formulate a detailed, step-by-step plan for their early twenties and will prefer to finish their education as quickly as possible. They will look for schools that welcome recent graduates. Others will want to take a year or two off and do something entirely unrelated before returning to graduate school. Admissions committees that traditionally discourage applicants straight out of college—or that look unfavorably upon applicants who have taken a deliberate detour—may find themselves passing over some of the best-qualified Millennials.

In all fields of graduate education, this generation will want structure, supervision, and feedback. Employers in the workplace are noticing that these young graduates seek constant monitoring and positive reinforcement in their activities. This sort of coaching is uncommon in today's graduate-level education, where faculty expect substantial self-direction from graduate students, many of whom feel isolated and drift without supervision for months at a time. Uninvolved and absentee advisors will become more controversial, perhaps even unacceptable, during the Millennial student era.

Many Millennials in graduate and professional school will want to turn away from the competitive stress they have known for so long, turning instead toward a more balanced and community-oriented lifestyle. Some will want to pursue extracurriculars of the same sort they did throughout their high school and college years, albeit in a lower-stress and more recreational way. One can picture Millennial medical students forming a women's soccer league, education schools publishing newspapers, arts academies starting businesses. While activities of this sort may appear totally unrelated to the professional fields for which students are training, they can foster important creativity, team, and management skills.

The Millennial-era preponderance of women in undergraduate education is extending into the graduate years, especially in law, health care, education, and the social sciences. Meanwhile, business, science, and technology student bodies remain majority male. If Millennials stabilize or reverse the recent trends toward later marriages and first births—which could well happen—graduate and professional schools in feminizing fields will face increasing pressure to accommodate the needs of new mothers. This could be an additional consideration in any discussion about the appropriate length, cost, and debt burden of postgraduate degree programs.

For graduate and professional programs, even more than for undergraduate education, the core issue of the Millennial student era will be job placement. During their graduate or professional education, Millennials will expect their schools to provide opportunities for clinical work, apprenticeships, and career-related community service. Even more than for college graduates, the stakes will be very high when the time comes for the "first real job." Most graduate programs already provide substantial help for students in their employment searches, both for summer and permanent positions, but not many provide the structure that Millennials will want—or the accountability that Gen-X parents will eventually demand. The more job placement and earnings data a program can provide the better.

Implications for Development and Alumni Offices

Millennials will be a key generation of alumni, given the new stakes for America's colleges in an era of shifting reputations. The post-graduate attitudes and experiences of these young adults will cement new collegiate brand positions in place. Approached the right way, many will become active, engaged, lifelong members of a university community. Approached the wrong way, many could feel alienated and look elsewhere for community ties. Alumni relations staffs will have to carefully evaluate exactly what they wish to get out of Millennials once they leave the college gates.

Currently, colleges have five generations of living alumni: G.I.s, Silent, Boomers, Gen Xers, and Millennials. As the decades roll by, the ranks of alumni will gradually change in generational distribution—and character.

Boomers are now the dominant alumni attending twenty-fifth and thirty-fifth reunions. By the 2020s, Gen Xers will fill that role. By the 2040s, it will be the Millennials' turn.

Year	Alumni Reunion Year				
	10th	25th	35th	50th	60th
2005	Gen X	Boomer	Boomer	Silent	G.I.
2020	Millennial	Gen X	Gen X	Boomer	Silent
2035	Homeland[1]	Millennial	Gen X	Gen X	Boomer
2050	Homeland[1]	Millennial	Millennial	Gen X	Gen X

[1] Generation born after the Millennials, exact birthdates not yet known

Gen Xers will reach their twenty-fifth and thirty-fifth reunions just as the second half of Generation X is still sending its children off to college. Parents, applicants, public officials, and Gen-X alumni donors will demand data on the economic and career success obtained for the price of tuition — in other words, the value of a college's "product." While Gen-X parents will be the primary ones demanding this kind of accountability, Millennial alumni will be the ones who can best provide it. A university that starts collecting data on the postgraduate experience of recent alumni (fields, earnings, risks, family life, and so on), and continues to do so over the next few decades, will find itself in a stronger competitive position. With these data, a college can take charge of its own brand position by marketing to prospective students and their parents on its own terms.

Gathering this kind of data will require the participation of Millennial alumni. Colleges that maintain the right relationship with them will find them very willing to comply. More than Gen Xers or Boomers at that phase of life—especially if approached properly—Millennial young adults will take active roles in their college communities, spurred by their high level of institutional trust, close relationships with older people, and lifelong tendency to stay attached to their ever-expanding social networks. Just as today's collegians can be seen walking around campus, cell phone in hand, talking to tight groups of high school friends, one can imagine twentysomethings alumni using breaks on the job to call college friends. Many of these graduates will be inclined to feel pride in their institutions, return for reunions, and sustain ties with own special fraternities and sororities.

With such strong institutional loyalty and peer cohesion, Millennial alumni will be uniquely suited to strengthen employment networks, among themselves and for younger graduates. Those who settle close to their college can strengthen its ties with the local community through internships, externships, and other professional development programs. More than older generations, Millennial graduates can be counted on to donate their time to projects or events organized by a university and then mobilize in large groups to support these events. Service projects will also broadly appeal to them.

The increased female share of collegians will, in time, translate into an increased female share of influential alumni. As this happens, the image of the traditional alumni—and alumni event—will need to evolve, with greater emphasis on women's athletics, community service, and the arts. The greater ethnic diversity of Millennial alumni could create a new opportunity to involve alumni on an ongoing basis with a university's ethnic organizations and academic departments.

Even as the alumni population becomes less male and Caucasian, it will become increasingly cohesive, defined less by its fringes and more by its new trans-ethnic mainstream. Regardless of gender or ethnicity, Millennial alumni can be expected to appreciate old-fashioned homecomings, alumni weekends, and major athletic events that they can turn into mini-reunions and enjoy as a group.

Millennials will be very active, upbeat, and engaged alumni. That's the good news. The other news about Millennial alumni is this: They may be a very tough sell for institutional fund-raising. Alumni relations staffs can brace for difficulty in raising money directly from this generation.

Today's students are very conscious that they and their parents have already been asked to pay as much as $50,000 a year for college. This burden will keep some of them heavily in debt for the first ten or fifteen years of their professional lives, a far longer time than was true for prior generations of alumni. Much will depend of course on whether or how rapidly their salaries grow in inflation-adjusted dollars over the coming decades. In the mind of many

Millennial graduates, however, colleges will always seem more like creditors than benefactors—a perception that will not be conducive to opening their checkbooks, either while they are paying off their debts or later in life.

To understand this new Millennial perspective, consider the total lifetime contributions of any individual to a college as the sum of the tuition they pay as students plus the gifts they donate later as graduates. This dynamic has changed significantly over the past few generations. Recent fund-raising campaigns have targeted mostly Silent and Boomer alumni, who paid only a fraction of Millennial-era tuition in inflation-adjusted dollars. Even when a 72-year-old alumnus makes a $100,000 gift to an alma mater during a fiftieth reunion year, that individual's total lifetime contribution, tuition and gifts combined, will be less than what many a Millennial 25-year-old has already paid.

Gen Xers were the first generation to feel heavy financial pressure from higher education, having been students when tuitions rose steeply. As they reach the traditional age for major alumni donations, they will start questioning how much they really can—or should—"give back." Millennials have been even more burdened by high tuition and student loans than Gen X, and they are even more deeply aware of how these high costs are impacting their lives. One often hears recent college graduates express what may well be a lifelong resistance to college donations, the sentiment that they have already given as much (at least financially) as they are going to give.

As colleges try to fund-raise from Millennials, they would be wise to tailor their appeal in ways that fit this generation's collective sensibility. Rather than raising money for new constructions or other campus-based purposes, alumni campaigns could target classmates (or younger graduates) who are having difficulty coping with their debt burdens. One recent graduate told the media that, if he won the lottery, he would use the money to repay the student loans of his entire college class. As concerned as they are about the large income disparities among their own ranks, Millennials are likely to consider this kind of donation more useful than one that simply adds to an institutional endowment. Indeed, graduates of the most heavily endowed universities may wonder why none of this accumulated wealth was used to relieve their own heavy tuition burdens—and may see this as a further reason not to contribute.

As is true for every generation, Millennial alumni will have a lifelong relationship with their colleges and graduate schools. If universities approach them properly, offering the right activities and making the right requests, this relationship can be a positive and productive one for this generation and for the institutions themselves.

15 | The Next Great Collegiate Generation

"Every generation has its chance at greatness. Let this one take its shot."

— *NEWSWEEK* (2000)

The Next Great Collegiate Generation

Every generation has its own strengths and weaknesses, its own potential for triumph and tragedy. The course of human history affords to each generation an opportunity to apply its unique gifts for the benefit of others. Some generations steer their world toward outer-world rationality, others toward inner-world passion. Some focus on graceful refinement, others on the hardscrabble bottom line. The German historian Leopold von Ranke, who weighed many Old World generations on the scales of history, observed that "before God all the generations of humanity appear equally justified." In "any generation," he concluded, "real moral greatness is the same as in any other..."

What will Millennials provide for those who come after? It is this future contribution, not what they have done in youth, that will be their test of greatness.

The collective Millennial lifespan—and its influence on history—will stretch far into the Twenty-First Century. In 2004 the first cohorts graduated from college. In 2006 they began graduating from business and professional schools, in 2007 they will graduate from law schools, and in 2008–09 they will begin graduating from medical schools and Ph.D. programs. Over the next two decades, this generation will fill the ranks of young-adult celebrities in the Olympics, pro sports, and entertainment—and the ranks of the military in any wars the nation may wage. In 2007, the first Millennial women will reach the median age of first marriage and of giving birth to a first child. The first Millennial men will reach that age in 2009. The first Millennial college graduates, women and men, will reach those median ages about two years later than their generation as a whole—in 2009 and 2011, respectively. From now through 2020, they will make a major mark on the youth pop culture. A new youth activism will begin having real impact on national politics in the elections of 2008 and 2012.

Through the 2010s, Millennials will be giving birth in large numbers, returning to college for their fifth-year and tenth-year reunions—and swarming into business and the professions, no longer as apprentices. Some will enter state houses and the U.S. Congress. Around 2020, they will elect their first U.S. Senator—around 2030, their first U.S. President. In the 2020s, their first children will apply to college. In 2029 and 2039, they will attend their first twenty-fifth and thirty-fifth college reunions. They will occupy the White House into the 2050s, during which period they will also provide majorities in the Congress and Senate, win Nobel prizes, rule corporate board rooms, and fill the ranks of collegiate parent bodies. Thereafter, into the 2070s, they will occupy the Supreme Court and be America's new elders. And along the way, they will make lasting contributions to literature, science, technology, and many other fields. Their children will dominate American life in the latter half of the Twenty-First Century—and their grandchildren will lead us into the Twenty-Second. Their influence on the American story, and the memory of their deeds and collective persona, will reach far beyond the year 2100.

As is true for any generation, history will intrude on the Millennials' collective life story, posing distinct challenges and opportunities. How they respond will alter the way others see them and the way they see themselves. What would one have said about the future of the G.I. Generation of youth back in 1928, before World War II redefined who they were and how they lived their lives? What would one have said about the future of young Boomers back in 1962, before the Consciousness Revolution? And what of Generation X in 1979, before the digital age?

Towards the close of his re-nomination address in 1936, President Roosevelt said:

> *There is a mysterious cycle in human events.*
> *To some generations much is given.*
> *Of other generations much is expected.*
> *This generation of Americans has a rendezvous with destiny.*

When summoning "this generation" to a "rendezvous with destiny," Roosevelt may have been referring generally to all Americans alive at the time. In particular, he was referring to the G.I. Generation—those young men and women who had overwhelmingly voted him into office and who, within a few years, would rally behind his elder leadership with dedication, energy, courage, and intelligence. Together, all of America's adult generations—leaders, generals, and soldiers—fought and won a war civilization could not afford to lose, achieving a triumph we today honor with monuments and memorials.

Perhaps because we know them better than those two other World War II-era generations, we especially revere today's very old G.I. war veterans and their widows. As young people, the G.I.s understood how much older generations had given them. They wanted to give back, and they did—especially in World War II. Another way they gave back was to nurture a new postwar generation of idealistic Boomers. Those Boomers have given birth to the first Millennials, and the story continues.

The Millennials' greatness as a generation has yet to reveal itself. When the strengths of this generation do appear, it is unlikely they will resemble those of their Boomer parents. Instead, these virtues are more likely to call to mind the confidence, optimism, and civic spirit of the high-achieving G.I.s.

What will happen over the course of their lives is, of course, unknowable. It is possible Millennials will dominate the story of the Twenty-First Century to much the same degree as the G.I. Generation dominated the story of the twentieth. If Millennials face their own "rendezvous with destiny" as they come of age, much will be expected of them by older generations. Will future writers have reason to call them, on their record of achievement, another "great generation"? Time will tell.

As was true in Roosevelt's time, educators will play an important role in forming young people for whatever they may encounter. Beyond catering to Millennials' personal needs—in academics, in the workplace, in the culture, in families—educators can keep in mind what is likely to be required of them by history. Beyond considering their own aspirations, consider what will be expected of this rising generation by society, the nation, and the world—and what their own "rendezvous with destiny" might in fact be.

When we wrote *The Fourth Turning* in 1997, we forecast that, sometime in the current decade, America would enter a new societal mood of historical urgency, sacrifice, and renewal, an era of crisis, a "fourth turning" comparable in significance to the American Revolution, Civil War, and era spanning the Great Depression and World War II. We predicted that this shift would occur as Boomers entered the elder age brackets (holding national leadership), as Gen Xers entered midlife (managing businesses, public life, and culture), and as Millennials came of age (entering the workplace as young adults and politics as young activists). Today, these three generations are entering these new stages of life—and very much appear to be pushing America into a new era.

Much of what we forecast in 1997 is now coming to pass. In particular, American society is growing less tolerant of personal risk-taking and more tolerant of civic risk-taking, including war. If we do indeed move into a new "fourth turning," the next two decades could involve substantial tests of America's society and place in the world. This could include a protracted War on Terror, a crisis of weapons proliferation, economic disruptions, fiscal collapse, an energy shortage, an environmental crisis, new civil wars abroad, a culture-war end game here at home—or any combination of all these things.

Whatever challenges our nation and world may encounter in the years to come, the largest challenge and greatest call to sacrifice will be borne by the generation now coming of age. Millennials will see in this a lifetime agenda—an agenda that will sharpen the traits that already make them so unlike Boomers and Gen Xers.

The anxiety about a "fourth turning" is palpably on the rise among all three of these generations, each of whom will be a dominant player in the first half of the Twenty-First Century. In a recent speech about the War on Terrorism, President Bush said: "The war against this enemy is more than a military conflict. It is the decisive ideological struggle of the Twenty-First Century and the calling of our generation." Like Roosevelt on the eve of World War II, Bush described an era in which the larger tides of history converge to form the destiny of a generation. Unlike Roosevelt, Bush was clearly referring to his own generation of elder Boomers. As of yet, no leader has summoned Millennials to sacrifice, or summoned them to greatness, in the manner Roosevelt did. In time, this could happen.

Whatever history's challenge—whether economic, political, military, social, or environmental—Millennials may provide just what those times will require. Perhaps they will mobilize to meet it with the upbeat attitude, can-do confidence, and civic spirit that will enhance the prospects for a successful outcome. Whatever the crisis, Millennials will realize that the bulk of their lives will lie in the years beyond it—while those who teach them will realize that the bulk of their lives has already transpired in the years before.

The graver the national peril, the more the nation will focus on this generation. What they need will become a national priority, what they suffer a source of national anguish, and what they achieve a source of national pride.

Today's older generations—parents, educators, and leaders—are preparing Millennials to face whatever history may hand them. This is perhaps the greatest service universities can accomplish in the decades ahead: to equip Millennials for their rendezvous with destiny.

As they engage in this task in the coming era, America's colleges and universities will forge new reputations, just as many of today's most prestigious colleges originally drew their reputations from the civic contributions of students and faculty during World War II. Institutions of higher learning will re-establish their mid-Twenty-First Century reputations based partly on what they will have provided for individual students, but also on what they will have provided for this generation as a whole, and how this helped Millennials and their nation triumph over whatever adversities lay in their paths.

Thus will the decades ahead be a time of historic opportunity for colleges and universities, as they help today's young people achieve greatness in their own time and generation.

Millennials are rising—and, with them, so may the service to history of higher education.

About the Authors

Neil Howe and William Strauss are best-selling authors, national speakers, and renowned authorities on generations in America. They have together written six books, all widely used by businesses, colleges, government agencies, and political leaders of both parties. Their blend of social science and history—and their in-depth analysis of American generations—lend order, meaning, and even a measure of predictability to social change.

Their first book, *Generations* (Morrow, 1991), is a history of America told as a sequence of generational biographies. *Generations* has been photographed on Bill Clinton's White House desk, quoted approvingly by Rush Limbaugh and Newt Gingrich, used by Tony Robbins, and cited by economic forecasters from Harry Dent to David Hale. Then-Vice President Al Gore sent a copy to every Member of Congress, calling it, "the most stimulating book on American history I have ever read."

Their second book, *13th-Gen* (Vintage, 1993), remains the top selling non-fiction book on Generation X. *The Fourth Turning* (Broadway, 1997) forecast a major mood change in America shortly after the new millennium—a change much like what actually happened after September 11, 2001. *The Fourth Turning* reached number ten on the *amazon.com* list four years after its release, and its web site (fourthturning.com) hosts the internet's longest-running discussion forum for any nonfiction book. "We will never be able to think about history in the same way," declared public opinion guru Dan Yankelovich.

Millennials Rising (Vintage, 2000) has been widely quoted in the media for its insistence that today's new crop of teens and kids are very different from Generation X and, on the whole, doing much better than most adults think. "Forget Generation X—and Y, for that matter," says the *Washington Post*, "The authors make short work of most media myths that shape our perceptions of kids these days." According to *The Chronicle of Higher Education*, "Administrators say they can already see indicators of the trends predicted by the authors." "The book is stuffed with interesting nuggets," wrote the *New York Times*. "It is brightly written. And it illuminates changes that really do seem to be taking place." "It's hard to resist the book's hopeful vision for our children and future," added *NEA Today*, "Many of the theories they wrote about in their two previous books—*Generations* and *13th-Gen*—have indeed come to pass." The most recent Howe-Strauss book, *Millennials and the Pop Culture* (LifeCourse, 2006), applies the same generational insights and methodologies to the entertainment industry that this book does to academe.

Articles by Howe and Strauss have appeared in the *Atlantic*, the *Washington Post*, the *New York Times*, *American Demographics*, *USA Today*, *USA Weekend*, and other national publications.

The Strauss-Howe theories and predictions are based on their profiles of generations—each reflecting distinct values formed during the eras in which its members grew up and came of age. The authors have observed that similar generational profiles recur in cycles driven by a rhythmic pattern of non-linear shifts, or "turnings," in America's social mood. This cyclical pattern has been present for centuries, and not just in America. History shapes generations, and then generations shape history.

William Strauss's first book, *Chance and Circumstance* (1978) is a widely acclaimed history of the Vietnam draft. Strauss is also a noted playwright, theater director, and performer. He is co-founder and director of the professional satirical troupe Capitol Steps. The Steps have released twenty-six albums (most recently, *I'm So Indicted*), two books (*Fools on the Hill* and *Sixteen Scandals*), and have performed numerous times off-Broadway with Strauss in the cast. Strauss has written three musicals (*MaKiddo*, *Free-the-Music.com*, and *Anasazi*) and two plays (*Gray Champions* and *The Big Bump*) about themes in the books he has co-authored with Howe. In the summer of 1999, he co-founded the Cappies, now an international "Critics and Awards" program for high school students (www.cappies.com). In 2005–06, he advised a creative team of high school students who wrote the new musical *Edit:Undo* (www.

editundo.org). Strauss holds graduate degrees from Harvard Law School and the Kennedy School of Government. He lives in McLean, Virginia, with his wife Janie. They have four grown children.

Neil Howe is senior associate at the Center for Strategic and International Studies, senior advisor to the Concord Coalition (where he co-authors a quarterly newsletter on the federal budget), and advisor on public policy to the Blackstone Group. Howe has written extensively on budget policy and aging and on attitudes toward economic growth, social progress, and stewardship. He previously coauthored *On Borrowed Time* (1989; reissued 2004), a pioneering call for budgetary reform. He has drafted several Social Security reform plans and testified on entitlements many times before Congress. Howe coauthors numerous publications for the Global Aging Initiative at CSIS, including studies on demographic change in China and Europe. He holds graduate degrees in history and economics from Yale University. He lives in Great Falls, Virginia, with his wife Simona and two children, Giorgia and Nathaniel.

About LifeCourse Associates

LifeCourse Associates is a generational consulting firm developed by Howe and Strauss in response to the many inquiries resulting from their books. They offer keynote speeches, seminars, communications products, generational audits, and consultations that apply the authors' unique historical analysis to help audiences better understand their businesses, families, and personal futures. Their ideas and generational perspective can be useful for strategic planning, marketing, product development, communications, and human resources.

The U.S. Department of Labor and U.S. Department of Health and Human Services have adopted the Howe-Strauss generational framework. Other LifeCourse clients have included Viacom (including MTV, Nickelodeon, and Paramount Pictures), the U.S. Marine Corps, Ford Motor Company, Procter and Gamble, Mercer Consulting, PBS, Nike, AARP, Scholastic, Inc., Northrop Grumman, Merrill Lynch, Walt Disney, the National Hockey League, and the U.S. Bureau of the Census, among many others. Howe and Strauss have spoken to the faculty and administrators of many K-12 school systems, community colleges, and universities—and to such national higher education organizations as the American Association of Collegiate Registrars and Admissions Officers (AACRAO), the National Association of College Admissions Counselors (NACAC), and the Council of Independent Colleges (ICI), among many others.

To contact LifeCourse Associates
call (866) 537-4999
or go to www.lifecourse.com

Sources

Given the vast range of topics covered in this book—and the numberless scholarly, journalistic, and pop culture sources that bear some connection to them—there is no way to reference everything of interest. Readers who wish to dig deeper into the data sources for the behavior and attitude trends described here should consult the comprehensive bibliographic reference section included at the end of *Millennials Rising* (2001). As a convenience, a brief list is provided here of the sources (from publications and web sites to programs and agencies) that were of particular use in preparing this book.

Readers who want to find out more about the Strauss-Howe generational perspective on American history, or about the authors' earlier treatments of the Millennial Generation, are invited to read the authors' three previous books: *Generations* (1991), *13th-Gen* (1993), and *The Fourth Turning* (1997).

Readers with further questions are invited to contact the authors at LifeCourse Associates, by emailing authors@lifecourse.com.

Sources on Behavior, Summary List

General
The Child and Family Web Guide (Tufts University), web site
Child Trends DataBank (Child Trends), web site
America's Children (U.S. Federal Interagency Forum on Child
    and Family Statistics), annual publication
Trends in the Well-Being of America's Children and Youth (U.S.
    Department of Health and Human Services), 2003
The State of America's Children (Children's Defense Fund), annual publication

Demographics, Family Structure, Race, Ethnicity, Family Income
U.S. Bureau of the Census
U.S. Bureau of Labor Statistics (Department of Labor)

Youth Employment

What Is Happening to Youth Employment Rates? (Congressional Budget Office), 2004

Educational Achievement

National Assessment of Educational Progress, "The Nation's Report Card"
(U.S. Department of Education), regular publications and web site
Rising to the Challenge: Are High School Graduates Prepared for College and Work?
(Achieve, Inc.), 2005
High School Survey of Student Engagement (Indiana University School of Education),
annual publication

Schools & Colleges

The College Board, web site and publications (e.g.: *Trends in Student
Aid, Trends in College Pricing, Education Pays,* 2006)
The Condition of Education (U.S. National Center for Education Statistics,
U.S. Department of Education), annual publication and web site
Report draft (Commission on the Future of Higher Education,
U.S. Department of Education), 2006
Reality Check: How Black and Hispanic Families Rate Their Schools
(Education Insights at Public Agenda), 2006
The Silent Epidemic: Perspectives of High School Dropouts
(Bill & Melinda Gates Foundation), 2006

Children's Use of Time

Sandra L. Hofferth and Jack Sandberg, *Changes in American Children's Time, 1981–1997*
(Institute for Social Research and Population Studies Center, University of Michigan), 1998

Youth Health & Risk Behaviors

U.S. National Center for Health Statistics
Youth Risk Behavior Surveillance System (U.S. Centers for Disease Control and
Prevention), web site and *National Youth Risk Behavior Survey: 1991–2005,* 2006
U.S. National Institute of Child Health and Human Development (National
Institutes of Health, Department of Health and Human Services)
Youth Studies Group (Stanford Center for Research in Disease Prevention)

Teen Births, Abortions

U.S. National Center for Health Statistics
Alan Guttmacher Institute, publications and web site

Family Dysfunction

U.S. Children's Bureau (Administration on Children, Youth and Families, of the
Administration for Children and Families, Department of Health and Human Services)
U.S. National Center on Child Abuse and Neglect (Administration on
Children, Youth and Families, of the Administration for Children
and Families, Department of Health and Human Services)

Youth Drug Abuse

U.S. Substance Abuse and Mental Health Services Administration (Department of Health and Human Services), regular publications and web site

Lloyd D. Johnston, Jerald G. Bachman, and Patrick M. O'Malley (project directors), Monitoring the Future Study (Institute for Social Research, University of Michigan), annual questions to students in grades 12 (since the class of 1975) and in grades 10 and 8 (since the class of 1991); reports issued in various years

Partnership for a Drug Free America, publications and web site

Youth Crime

U.S. National Criminal Justice Reference Service (Department of Justice), publications and web site

National School Safety Center, publications and web site

Sources on Attitudes, Summary List

America's Promise

Voices Study: Research Findings (America's Promise), 2005

Drexel Poll

Drexel University Futures Poll: Teenagers, Technology and Tomorrow (Drexel University), 1997

Gallup Polls

Gallup News Service (The Gallup Organization) web site

Generation 2001

Generation 2001 Survey (Northwestern Mutual Life), 1999

Generational Marketing

American Demographics, periodical

Horatio Alger

The State of Our Nation's Youth (Horatio Alger Association), annual publication and web site

Monitoring the Future

Lloyd D. Johnston, Jerald G. Bachman, and Patrick M. O'Malley (project directors), Monitoring the Future Study (Institute for Social Research, University of Michigan), annual questions to students in grades 12 (since the class of 1975) and in grades 10 and 8 (since the class of 1991); reports issued in various years

Phi Delta Kappa

Lowell C. Rose and Alec M. Gallup, *The 38th Annual Phi Delta Kappa/Gallup Poll of the Public's Attitudes Toward the Public Schools*, 2006

NASSP

The Mood of American Youth (National Association of Secondary School Principals), 1974, 1983, and 1996; students aged 13–17 interviewed early in each year

Pew Center

The Pew Research Center for the People and the Press, regular published surveys on youth (e.g., *Motherhood Today—A Tougher Job*, Less Ably Done, 1997)

Primedia/Roper

The PRIMEDIA/Roper National Youth Opinion Survey (PRIMEDIA, Inc., and Roper Starch Worldwide, Inc.), 1998; students in grades 7–12 interviewed in Nov, 1998

Public Agenda

Public Agenda, regular published surveys on youth attitudes and adult attitudes toward youth (e.g., *Life After High School: Young People Talk about Their Hopes and Prospects*, 2005).

Roper Youth Report

Roper Youth Report (Roper Starch Worldwide), annual publication, results reported irregularly
Shell Poll
The Shell Poll (Shell Oil Company), 1999

TRU

Teenage Research Unlimited, posted news releases on web site

UCLA Freshman Poll

L.J. Sax, A.W. Astin, W. S. Korn, and K.M. Mahoney, *The American Freshman* (Higher Education Research Institute, University of California at Los Angeles), published annually, yearly surveys since 1966

Who's Who

Annual Survey of High Achievers (Who's Who Among American High School Students), "high-achieving" high school student interviewed annually since 1967; web site

YATS

Youth Attitude Tracking Survey (Defense Manpower Data Center, U.S. Department of Defense), survey of potential high school-aged recruits, published annually